joyful Daily Stitching
seam by seam

Complete Guide to 500 Embroidery-Stitch Combinations
Perfect for Crazy Quilting

Valerie Bothell

C&T PUBLISHING

PUBLISHER: Amy Marson

CREATIVE DIRECTOR: Gailen Runge

EDITORS: Liz Aneloski and Katie Van Amburg

TECHNICAL EDITOR: Helen Frost

COVER/BOOK DESIGNER: April Mostek

PRODUCTION COORDINATOR: Tim Manibusan

PRODUCTION EDITOR: Jennifer Warren

ILLUSTRATOR: Mary E. Flynn

PHOTO ASSISTANT: Mai Yong Vang

HAND MODEL: Kristi Visser

PHOTOGRAPHY by Diane Pedersen of C&T Publishing, Inc., unless otherwise noted

Published by C&T Publishing, Inc., P.O. Box 1456, Lafayette, CA 94549

Library of Congress Cataloging-in-Publication Data

Names: Bothell, Valerie, 1962- author.

Title: Joyful daily stitching, seam by seam : complete guide to 500 embroidery-stitch combinations, perfect for crazy quilting / Valerie Bothell.

Description: Lafayette, CA : C&T Publishing, Inc., 2017. | Includes bibliographical references.

Identifiers: LCCN 2017030793 | ISBN 9781617455513 (soft cover)

Subjects: LCSH: Stitches (Sewing) | Crazy quilts.

Classification: LCC TT705 .B66 2017 | DDC 746.46/041--dc23

LC record available at https://lccn.loc.gov/2017030793

Printed in the USA

10 9 8 7 6 5 4 3 2 1

Dedication

With needle and thread

Her soft heart that was tattered

Was mended again.

This book is dedicated to all whose heart may need a little mending here and there. May God bless you with a peace that passes understanding.

A Mended Heart, 20″ × 20″, by Valerie Bothell, 2016

Acknowledgments

This book is a culmination of many years of stitching, and I would like to thank my family for supporting me by giving me the time to stitch daily. (My boys have spent many hours watching their mom "play with her ribbons.") I would like to thank Jacob Bothell for the beautiful author photo he took for me and Craig Bothell for the many glasses of ice tea he brought me.

I have many friends who inspired me and supported me as I wrote this book. A special thank-you to Andrea Hankins, who came along and picked me up at just the right time—that means so much to me. Many thanks also to the members of my Bible study: Peggy Collins and her girls Lindsay, Candice, Shelly, Shiloh, Norma Ward, Donna Glanville, and Jillian Hurst.

A very special thank-you to Amy Marson, Roxane Cerda, and Liz Aneloski for seeing my vision for this book and giving me the chance to make it come to life. I feel honored.

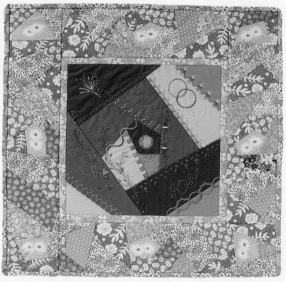

Joyful Beginnings, 17″ × 17″, by Valerie Bothell, 2015

Many thanks to Judith Baker Montano and Carole Samples for inspiring me many years ago when I started to crazy quilt.

And to God, who makes all things possible.

Contents

Introduction

Welcome to the wonderful world of joyful embellishments!

I have been a crazy quilter for over twenty years—I never get tired of it! My eye has always been drawn to different embroidery stitches used in vintage quilts. I love to see how creative quilters were with their needle and thread.

Several years ago, I had the opportunity to view one of the best-known crazy quilts, *My Crazy Dream*, which is owned by the International Quilt Study Center & Museum in Lincoln, Nebraska. It was made by Mary M. Hernandred Ricard between the years of 1877 and 1912. There were several things that surprised me about this crazy quilt, the main one being that it wasn't finished! There were places where the embroidery had been marked with a pencil but hadn't been completed. The stitching that is complete is beautiful, intricate, and creative—all things that I admire.

When I talk about making crazy quilts, people often seem to think that crazy quilting is too time-consuming, a lot of work, and maybe not even worth the effort. Then I think about Mary Ricard working on a crazy quilt for more than 35 years. Why did she spend so much time on that quilt? The answers may vary for each quilter, but I know why I work on crazy quilts: because I love it and it soothes my soul.

Several years ago, I went through a fairly tough time and decided to challenge myself by making a crazy quilt in which every seam would have a different stitch combination. I started with a center section composed of 9 pink blocks. The quilt kept growing with the addition of a bright green border with 16 blocks. About 6 months later, I decided to add an outer purple border with 24 blocks.

At first the project seemed overwhelming, but I decided to think about it in smaller increments. I am very goal oriented, so I did the math. I realized that if I did 1 seam a day for 5 days a week, I would have a little over 250 seams done by the end of 1 year!

As I stitched on my blocks every day and completed the goals I had made for myself, the tough time faded away; my heart began to heal. I also ended up with a beautiful crazy quilt composed of 49 blocks and 500 different stitch combinations.

It is my hope that, as you make your way through the stitches in this book, you will find joy—and healing, if needed—by taking the time to do a little stitching every day.

—*Valerie Bothell*

Crazy Quilt Piecing

The 49 blocks included in my crazy quilt were made using the Montano Centerpiece Method. In addition to this method, I have also included the Montano Fan Method as an option if you would like to mix the two different piecing methods in your quilt. I made each block 6½˝ × 6½˝ so that I could easily take them with me in a small bag.

montano centerpiece method

1. Cut a 5-sided fabric shape, and pin it right side up in the center of a muslin square.

2. Cut a rectangular piece that fits on one side of the center fabric.

3. Pin the rectangular piece wrong side up, aligning it with the straight edge. Sew with an ⅛˝ seam allowance. Press open.

4. Working clockwise, cut the next piece of fabric. It should be long enough to cover the rectangular piece of fabric and the next side of the 5-sided shape.

5. Pin the piece wrong side up and sew with an ⅛˝ seam allowance. Trim the excess fabric from the seam and press open.

> **TIP**
> To make the block more interesting, start cutting different fabric shapes other than the rectangular shape you started with.

6. Repeat Steps 2–5 for the third, fourth, and fifth sides of the 5-sided shape.

7. Continue working clockwise until you have completely covered the muslin.

> **TIP**
> It is always a good idea to repeat some fabrics a couple of times in a block. Strategically place them so that the block looks balanced.

8. Trim the outside edges even with the muslin square. Sew around the perimeter of the block ⅛″ from the edge. This keeps the outer edges of the fabric in place.

TIP

You can give a block a "crazier" look by sewing together two pieces of fabric and then treating them as one piece when you sew them in place.

montano fan method

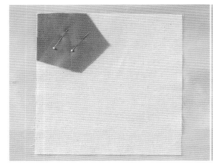

1. Cut a 5-sided fabric shape with a 90° corner. Pin it to the upper left corner of a muslin square, right side up.

2. Working clockwise, cut a rectangular piece that fits on the top right raw edge of the 5-sided shape. Pin the rectangular piece wrong side up, aligning it with the straight edge of the 5-sided shape. Sew an ⅛″ seam allowance. Press open.

TIP

To make the block more interesting, start cutting different fabric shapes other than the rectangular shape you started with.

3. Cut a third piece of fabric. It should be long enough to cover the previous rectangular piece of fabric and align with the next side of the 5-sided shape. (Some of the rectangle will extend beyond this new piece and will be trimmed later.) Pin the piece wrong side up and sew with an ⅛″ seam allowance. Trim the excess fabric from the seam of the previous piece, and press open.

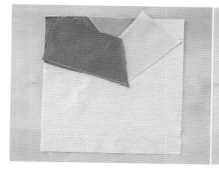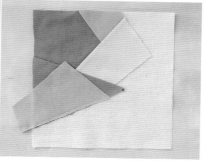

4. Cut a fourth piece of fabric long enough to cover the bottom edge of the first corner piece. Pin into place on the right edge, and sew with an ⅛" seam allowance. Trim the excess fabric from the seam and press open.

5. Working *counterclockwise*, cut a piece of fabric to cover part of the bottom edge of the piece you attached in Step 4. Pin in place, and sew with an ⅛" seam allowance. Trim the excess fabric from the seam and press open.

6. Cut another piece of fabric long enough to cover most of the bottom edges of the last 2 pieces that you added. Pin in place, and sew with an ⅛" seam allowance. Trim the excess fabric from the seam and press open.

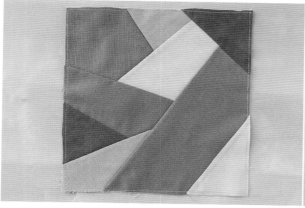

7. Continue piecing the block counterclockwise until you reach the right edge of the muslin square. When you reach the edge, begin to work *clockwise* until you have covered the muslin.

8. Trim the outside edges even with the muslin square. Sew around the perimeter of the block ⅛" from the edge.

> **TIP**
>
> You can give a block a "crazier" look by sewing together two pieces of fabric and then treating them as one piece when you sew them in place.

Hand Embroidery

hand-stitching tools

My love for hand stitching began at the age of eleven, when I found a red Christmas tin in the linen closet that was filled with embroidery floss. I started with simple projects, such as tea towels, and moved up to embroidering denim shirts, which was all the rage in those days.

Hand embroidery is relaxing; it is easy to take with you and work on wherever you go. The supplies are basic: threads, needles, scissors, and fabric or a crazy quilt block to work on. It always feels good to create something that is one of a kind. I tend to do most of my embroidering on crazy quilts, but it can also be used to dress up just about anything.

Needles

When choosing a needle for hand embroidery, there are four things I think about: the thread size, the type of project, the fabric the project is made of, and the type of embroidery stitches. For projects that are a single layer of fabric, such as an embroidery design done on muslin, an embroidery needle is the best choice. It is narrow and has a sharp point, and the shaft is elongated.

For crazy quilt embroidery, a chenille needle is what I reach for. It is wider, has a bigger eye, and has a sharp point to go through multiple layers of fabric. It is also the best choice if you are using a heavier thread, metallic thread, or silk ribbon. My favorite chenille needle sizes are #22 and #24.

For bullion embroidery, a milliners needle is the best choice. It has an elongated shaft, which gives you room to wrap the thread around the needle, and a smaller eye to make pulling the thread off the needle easier.

Needles come in different sizes; the smaller the number, the larger the eye of the needle. The needle size you should use is determined by your thread size. The thread should slide easily through the eye of the needle. If you are having problems pulling the thread through the fabric, you may need a larger needle size. The eye of a needle is made to thread from one side, so if you are having trouble threading a needle, try turning it to the other side.

Thread and Fabric Choices

When making thread choices, I think about the types of fabrics I am using. A wool project requires a heavier thread such as #5 or #8 perle cotton, but if I am working on silk, I use a finer thread such as a #12 perle cotton or a silk twist. There are many beautiful threads to choose from, but my favorites tend to be hand-dyed cottons or silks.

For my crazy quilt *Joyful Embellishments*, I chose Robert Kaufman's Kona Cotton solids. My emphasis for this project was the stitches, so I didn't want any kind of printed fabrics to distract from them. In other crazy quilt projects I have used all kinds of silks, satins, and velvets. I let some of the prints in the fabric become part of the design. For a more casual project, you may even want to try embroidering on denim.

The best advice I can give you for your thread and fabric choices is this: Use what you love! Then you will love what you are doing.

Hoop

When I work on a project that is a single layer of fabric, such as an embroidery design on muslin, I use a Q-Snap frame. They come in different sizes, and there are clamps that fit on the frame to keep the fabric taut. Pick a size that fits comfortably in your hands. If a hoop is too large, it can be difficult to reach to the center. For larger projects, use a smaller hoop and move it around on the project. When you are done embroidering, it is a good idea to remove the hoop to avoid getting permanent creases in the project.

When I embroider on a crazy quilt block, I don't use a hoop because I feel that the thickness of the fabrics gives the project enough stability on which to embroider.

even stitch tips

I love to make my stitches as even as possible—it's just the way I am! Over the years, I have found a few things that make my life simpler by helping me stitch more quickly without agonizing over every single stitch.

Tiger Tape

One of my favorite secret weapons is Tiger Tape. This is a tape that quilters use to make their stitches even when they are hand quilting. Tiger Tape comes in different widths and stitch sizes.

Chevron Stitch using Tiger Tape. Notice that not only can you make the diagonal line even by counting over four dashes but that you can make the bar on the top consistently the same size.

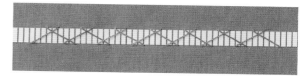

Herringbone Stitch using Tiger Tape

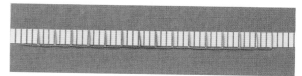

Blanket Stitch using Tiger Tape

One word of caution: Tiger Tape should not be used on velvets. Pulling off the tape pulls out the tufts of velvet. Trust me, I know from personal experience!

Crazy Quilt Grid Templates

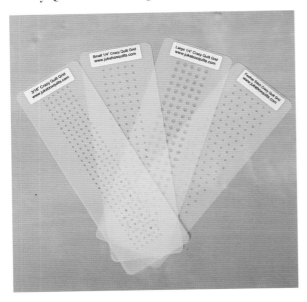

Crazy quilt grid templates have also made my stitching so much easier. My usual marking pen is a purple air-erasable marker. I also like to use fabric pencils (such as those by Collins or Sewline), depending on the project.

Note: For demonstrational purposes, I used a water-erasable pen in the photos. I never use them on a regular basis, as many of the fabrics I work with would not look good after getting wet!

Lay the template on the fabric and mark the dots with an air-erasable pen. Stitch your chosen embroidery stitch as usual, using the dots as a guide.

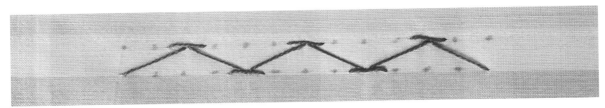

Chevron Stitch using crazy quilt grid templates

Herringbone Stitch using crazy quilt grid templates

Blanket Stitch using crazy quilt grid templates

embroidery transfer

There are many ways to transfer embroidery patterns so that you can stitch to your heart's delight.

If the pattern is small: Tape the embroidery design to a window, and tape quilting paper or vellum paper (such as Golden Threads quilting paper or Simple Foundations Translucent Vellum Paper by C&T Publishing) on top of it. Trace the design onto the quilting paper or vellum; then baste the design into place on the project.

If the pattern is big: Traditionally, you can trace the whole image by hand onto paper such as Golden Threads quilting paper or Simple Foundations Translucent Vellum Paper, but I found I really didn't want to spend a lot of time doing that. I came up with a quick solution using a copier, freezer paper, and quilting paper or vellum paper (such as those mentioned above).

1. Cut both the freezer paper and the Golden Threads quilting paper to 8½″ × 11″.

2. Iron the quilting paper to the shiny or slick side of the freezer paper, making sure there are no air bubbles.

3. Copy the pattern by running the freezer/quilting paper through a copier as usual.

4. Let the ink dry. Carefully remove the quilting paper from the freezer paper.

5. Baste the copy of the embroidery pattern in place on the block or fabric.

Vellum paper (such as Simple Foundations Translucent Vellum Paper by C&T Publishing) goes through a copier without using freezer paper. Let the ink dry before basting the embroidery pattern in place on the block or fabric.

Embroidery Stitches

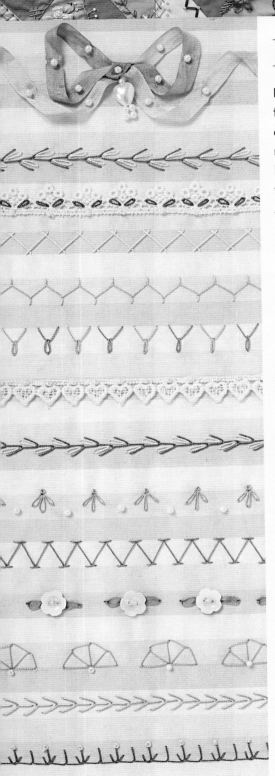

I love everything about crazy quilting, but hands down my favorite part is the hand embroidery! For me, hand embroidery is the great reward after doing all the piecing, and it really begins to "dress up" a crazy quilt block. What might look like a plain, ordinary block can turn into a real treasure when you spend a little time doing some handwork.

When I taught my *Crazy Quilt Stitch Sampler* to my students several years ago, I thought a piece of striped fabric would make it easier to learn the stitches. The stripes simulate seamlines on a crazy quilt block, so this is a good way to practice the stitches. All the stitches are demonstrated on striped fabric; you may do this as you practice, or you can start on a crazy quilt seam.

Crazy Quilt Stitch Sampler, 10″ × 13″, by Valerie Bothell

When working on the stitches, I encourage you to try combining the stitches in different ways. You can use different stitches to create a seam with dimension by building the seam up one stitch at a time.

Starting with a basic Feather Stitch, add Lazy Daisy Stitches, pearls, and Ribbon Stitches to create more interest in the stitch.

crazy quilt stitches

Back Stitch

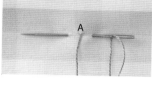

1. Bring up the needle on the edge of the stripe or crazy quilt seam at A. Take a stitch to the left, as shown.

2. Pull the needle to the front of the fabric. Move the needle to the right, and take a stitch back to A, using the same hole that was made in Step 1. In the same movement, take a stitch to the left, as shown.

3. Continue as needed.

TIP

The Back Stitch is very versatile, and I use it for many different applications. When I use it to outline an object or a monogram, I make my stitches smaller than when I use it as a base in combination stitches.

Blanket Stitch

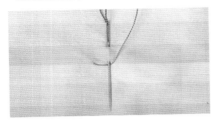

----- TIP -----

You can change the look of all the different Blanket Stitch forms by varying the width, height, and angle of the stitch. Experiment and see what different looks you can come up with.

1. Bring up the needle on the lower edge of the stripe or crazy quilt seam. Move the needle to the right, placing it in a perpendicular position. Make sure the thread is *under* the needle, as shown.

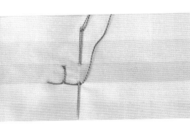

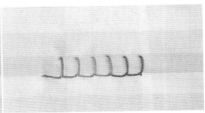

2. Pull the needle out of the fabric, and gently pull the thread to the right. Hold it in place with your left thumb.

3. Move the needle to the right, and take a stitch in the same manner as you did before.

4. Continue as needed.

Blanket Stitch—Beaded 1

For this stitch, use a needle with an eye big enough for the thread but small enough to go through the hole of the bead. An embroidery needle usually works well for this purpose.

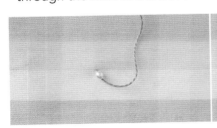

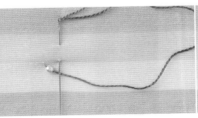

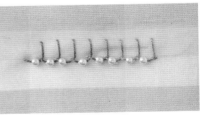

1. Bring up the needle on the lower edge of the stripe or crazy quilt seam, and string a bead on the thread.

2. Move the needle to the right, placing it in a perpendicular position. Make sure the thread is *under* the needle and the bead is to the left of the needle.

3. Continue as needed.

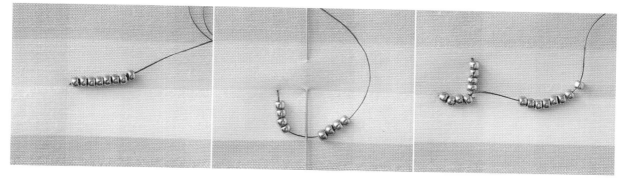

Blanket Stitch—Beaded 2

For demonstrational purposes, I used red beading thread to make it easier to see the stitch. Normally I use a thread that matches either the fabric or the bead, depending on the project.

1. Bring up the needle on the lower edge of the stripe or crazy quilt seam, and string 8 beads on the thread.

2. Move the needle to the right, placing it in a perpendicular position. Make sure that the thread is *under* the needle and that there are 4 beads to the left of the needle and 4 to the right.

3. Pull the needle to the front of the fabric, and string 8 more beads on the thread. Repeat Step 2.

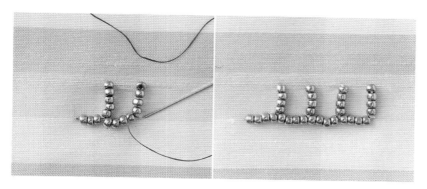

4. Continue as needed, taking the needle to the back of the fabric just on the other side of the thread that formed the last loop.

Blanket Stitch—Circular

For demonstrational purposes, I used a pen to mark my circle; normally I use a purple air-erasable pen that fades away after I finish stitching.

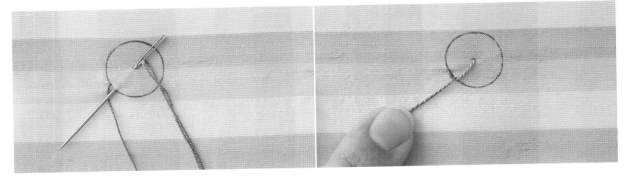

1. Draw a circle on the fabric and mark the center. Bring up the needle on the outer edge of the circle, and take a stitch from the center mark, moving the needle under the fabric to the outer edge of the circle. Make sure the thread is *under* the needle.

2. Pull the thread away from the circle until the stitch lies flat on the fabric. Keep consistent tension on the thread. If you pull the thread too hard, the fabric will pucker; if you leave it too loose, the stitches won't have a crisp look.

3. Continue around the circle, using the same hole in the center for each stitch until there is one last stitch to complete it. Place the needle under the thread from the first stitch; then take the needle to the back of the fabric in the center hole. *Make sure not to pull too tightly, or you will distort the circle.*

Blanket Stitch—Closed

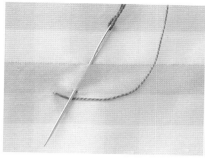 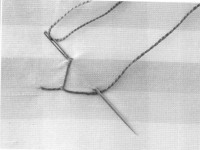 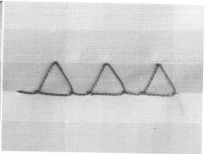

1. Bring up the needle on the lower edge of the stripe or crazy quilt seam. Take a stitch to the right, placing it at an angle. Make sure the thread is *under* the needle, as shown.

2. Pull the needle out of the fabric, and gently pull the thread to the right. Hold it in place with your left thumb, as shown in Blanket Stitch, Step 2 (page 16). Take a stitch to the right, placing it at an angle to make the 2 stitches come to a point. Take a stitch in the same manner as before.

3. Continue as needed.

Blanket Stitch—Crossed

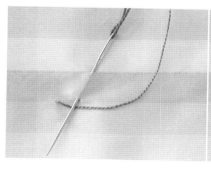 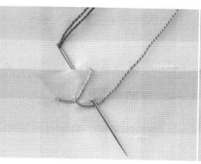 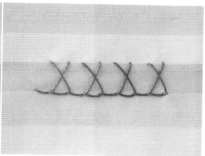

1. Bring up the needle on the lower edge of the stripe or crazy quilt seam. Take a stitch to the right, placing it at an angle. Make sure the thread is *under* the needle, as shown.

2. Pull the needle out of the fabric, and gently pull the thread to the right. Hold it in place with your left thumb, as shown in Blanket Stitch, Step 2 (page 16). Take a stitch to the right, placing it at an angle to make the 2 stitches cross. Take a stitch in the same manner as before.

3. Continue as needed.

Blanket Stitch—Fan

For demonstrational purposes, I used a pen to mark my fan shape; normally I use a purple air-erasable pen that fades away after I finish stitching.

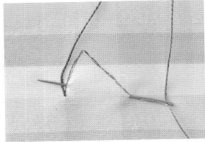 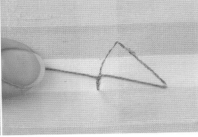 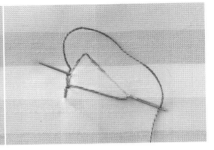

1. Draw a fan shape on the fabric. Bring up the needle on the fan's lower outer edge, and take a stitch from the end of the fan's slanted line, moving the needle under the fabric to the fan's outer edge. Make sure the thread is *under* the needle.

2. Pull the thread away from the fan until the stitch lies flat on the fabric. Keep consistent tension on the thread. If you pull the thread too hard, the fabric will pucker; if you leave it too loose, the stitches won't have a crisp look.

3. Continue stitching the fan shape. When taking the stitch at the end of the fan's slanted line, get as close to the first stitch as possible without crossing the threads.

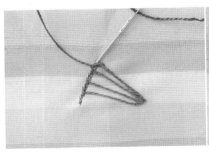 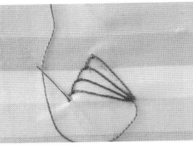 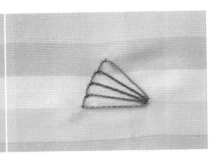

4. When the fan shape is complete, take the needle to the back of the fabric just on the other side of the thread that formed the last Blanket Stitch.

5. To complete the fan shape's lower edge, bring up the needle up just below the first stitch done at the end of the slanted line. Take the needle to the back of the fabric where the first stitch was started on the fan shape's lower edge.

Blanket Stitch—Knotted

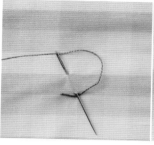 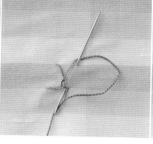 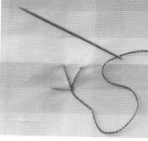 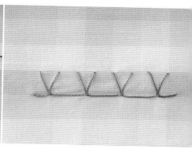

1. Bring up the needle on the lower edge of the stripe or crazy quilt seam. Take a stitch to the right, placing it at an angle. Make sure the thread is *under* the needle, as shown.

2. Take a stitch that starts at the base of the Blanket Stitch and angles to the right. Loop the thread around the needle. Make sure the thread is *under* the needle, as shown.

3. Pull the needle and thread toward you until the stitch lies flat on the fabric.

4. Continue as needed.

Blanket/Cretan Combination Stitch

Refer to Blanket Stitch (page 16) and Cretan Stitch (page 31) as needed.

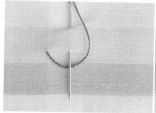 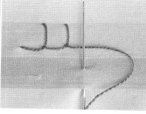 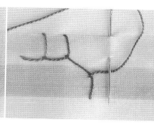

1. Bring up the needle on the lower edge of the stripe or crazy quilt seam. Move the needle to the right, and place it in a perpendicular position, with the needle going in a downward direction as you take the stitch. Make sure the thread is *under* the needle.

2. Repeat Step 1 to make another Blanket Stitch. Move the needle to the right, and place it in a perpendicular position on the opposite side of the striped fabric or seam, making sure the needle is moving in an upward direction as you take the stitch.

3. Move the needle to the right. Repeat Steps 1 and 2 as needed.

Blanket/Herringbone Combination Stitch

See Herringbone/Blanket Combination Stitch (page 41).

Bullion Knot

For this stitch, use a milliners needle in a size 3 or 5, depending on the size of the thread.

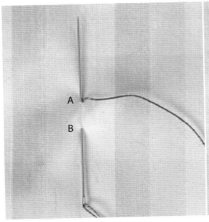
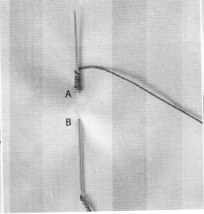
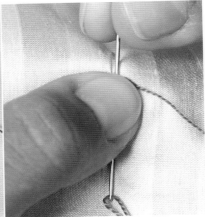

1. Pull the needle and thread to the front of the fabric at A. Take a stitch about ¼˝ to B, and push the tip of the needle to come out at A again, making sure not to pull the needle through the fabric. Holding the base of the needle and fabric in your left hand, push the tip of the needle up and away from the fabric. Pick up the thread coming out at A with your right hand.

2. Wrap the thread around the tip of the needle in a clockwise direction. The wraps around the needle need to be at least equal to the space between A and B.

3. When you have enough wraps on the needle, cover and hold the wraps with your left thumb. Pull the needle through the wraps with your right hand, pulling the thread in an upward motion until the bullion wraps are nearly down to the fabric.

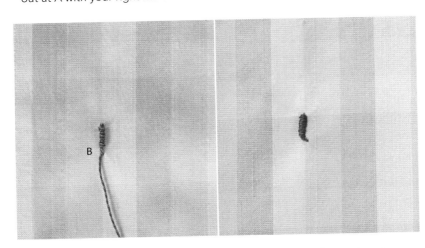

4. Pull the needle and thread toward B, laying the wraps flat against the fabric until there is no slack in the thread. Straighten any stray wraps by rubbing your finger over them until they lie smooth. Push the needle and thread to the back of the fabric at B.

Bullion Knot / Fly Stitch Combination Stitch

For this stitch, use a milliners needle in a size 3 or 5, depending on the size of the thread. Refer to Fly Stitch (page 38) and Bullion Knot (previous page) as needed.

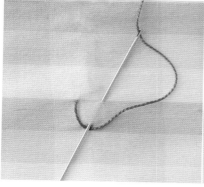
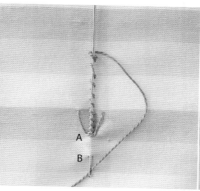
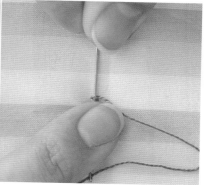

1. Bring the needle to the front of the fabric. Move the needle to the right; then slide it under the fabric at an angle. Make sure the thread is *under* the needle, as shown.

2. Pull the needle out from the fabric, and take a stitch about ¼″ to B. Push the tip of the needle to come out at A again, making sure not to pull the needle through the fabric. Make sure the needle is inside the loop that was formed in Step 1. Holding the base of the needle and fabric in your left hand, push the tip of the needle up and away from the fabric. Pick up the thread coming out at A with your right hand. Wrap the thread around the tip of the needle in a clockwise direction. The wraps around the needle need to be at least equal to the space between A and B.

3. When you have enough wraps on the needle, cover and hold the wraps with your left thumb. Pull the needle through the wraps with your right hand, pulling the thread in an upward motion until the bullion wraps are nearly down to the fabric.

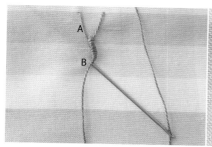
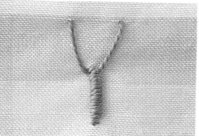

4. Pull the needle and thread toward B, laying the wraps flat against the fabric until there is no slack in the thread. Straighten any stray wraps by rubbing your finger over them until they lie smooth. Push the needle and thread to the back of the fabric at B.

Bullion Knot / Lazy Daisy Combination Stitch

For this stitch, use a milliners needle in a size 3 or 5, depending on the size of the thread. Refer to Bullion Knot (page 22) and Lazy Daisy (page 42) as needed.

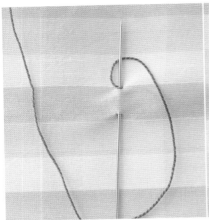

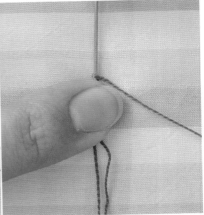

1. Bring up the needle on the edge of the stripe or crazy quilt seam. Take a stitch to the back of the fabric using the same hole, sliding the needle under the fabric. Make sure the thread is *under* the needle as it emerges from the fabric.

2. Wrap the thread around the tip of the needle in a clockwise direction 4 times.

3. When you have enough wraps on the needle, cover and hold the wraps with your left thumb. Pull the needle through the wraps with your right hand, pulling the thread in an upward motion until the bullion wraps are nearly down to the fabric.

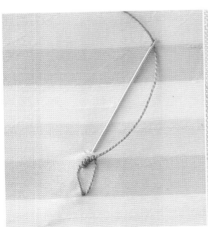

4. Take the needle to the back of the fabric, directly beneath where the thread emerges from the Bullion Knot that was just completed.

Chain Stitch

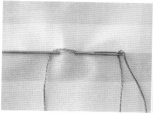

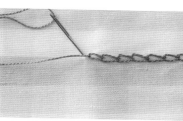

1. Bring up the needle on the edge of the stripe or crazy quilt seam. Take a stitch to the back of the fabric using the same hole, sliding the needle under the fabric.

2. Pull the thread to the front of the fabric, making sure the thread is *under* the needle, until the stitch forms a loop. You can control the shape of this loop by the amount of tension you have on the thread.

3. Take a stitch to the back of the fabric where the thread emerged from the last stitch, using the same hole and sliding the needle under the fabric. Repeat Step 2 until a loop forms.

4. Continue as needed. To end the stitch, take the needle to the back of the fabric just on the other side of the thread that formed the last loop.

Chain Stitch—Feathered

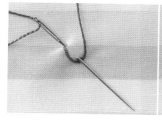

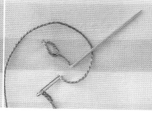
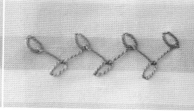

1. Bring up the needle on the upper edge of the stripe or crazy quilt seam. Take a stitch to the back of the fabric using the same hole, sliding the needle under the fabric at an angle.

2. Pull the thread to the front of the fabric, making sure the thread is *under* the needle, until the stitch forms a loop. You can control the shape of this loop by the amount of tension you have on the thread. Take the thread to the back of the fabric approximately ¼″ from where the thread emerged from the fabric.

3. Bring up the needle on the lower edge of the stripe or crazy quilt seam. Take a stitch to the back of the fabric using the same hole, sliding the needle under the fabric at an angle. Have the needle reemerge from the fabric very close to where the last stitch ended, making sure the thread is *under* the needle. Repeat Step 2.

4. Repeat Steps 2 and 3 as needed. Finish the last stitch by taking the needle to the back of the fabric just on the other side of the thread that formed the last stitch in Step 2.

Chain Stitch—Open

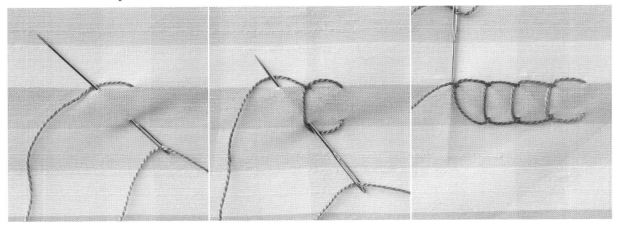

1. Bring up the needle on the upper edge of the stripe or crazy quilt seam. Below the first stitch, take a stitch at a 45° angle to the back of the fabric. Make sure that the thread is *under* the needle.

2. Pull the thread to the front of the fabric. Below where you emerged from the fabric, take a stitch at a 45° angle, making sure that the needle is inside the loop that was formed from the last stitch. Make sure that the thread is *under* the needle.

3. Repeat Step 2 as needed. To finish the stitch, take the needle to the back of the fabric just on the other side of the thread that formed the last loop. Make sure not to pull the loop too tight so that there will be enough thread to finish the loop correctly.

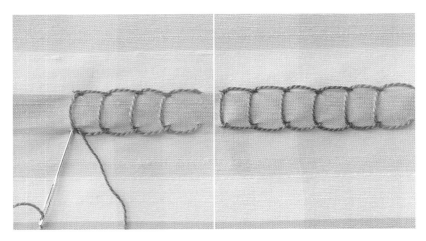

4. Bring up the needle below the last stitch, making sure that the shape of the loop looks the same as all the previous stitches. Take the needle to the back of the fabric just on the other side of the thread that formed the loop.

Chain Stitch—Open, Beaded

For demonstrational purposes, I used red beading thread to make it easier to see the stitch. Normally I use a thread that matches either the fabric or the bead, depending on the project.

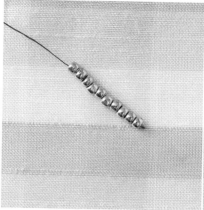
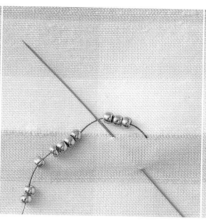
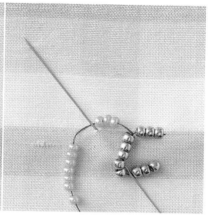

1. Bring the needle and thread up on the top edge of the stripe or crazy quilt seam. String 10 beads on the thread.

2. Take a stitch to the left at a 45° angle, making sure that 3 of the beads are to the right of the needle.

3. String 10 more beads on the thread. Take a stitch at a 45° angle from inside the loop of the first set of beads, making sure there are 3 beads to the right of the needle for both the first and second set of beads.

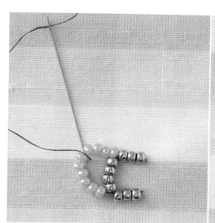
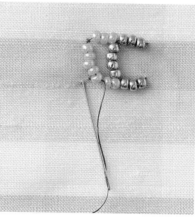

4. Repeat Step 3 as needed. To finish the stitch, bring the needle and thread to the front of the fabric inside the loop, making sure there are 3 beads to the right of the needle. Take the needle to the back of the fabric on the other side of the thread.

5. Bring up the needle on the lower edge of the stitch inside the loop, making sure there are 3 beads to the right of the needle; then take the needle to the back of the fabric on the other side of the thread.

Chain Stitch—Two Colors

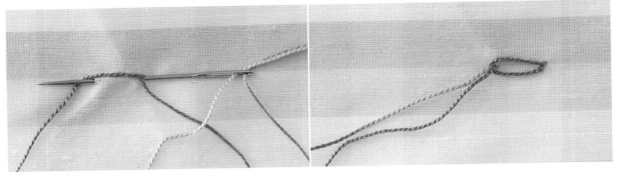

1. Thread the needle with 2 colors of thread. Bring up the needle on the edge of the stripe or crazy quilt seam, and take a stitch to the back of the fabric using the same hole, sliding the needle under the fabric. Loop one of the threads *under* the needle.

2. Pull the thread to the front of the fabric until the stitch forms a loop. You can control the shape of this loop by the amount of tension you have on the thread.

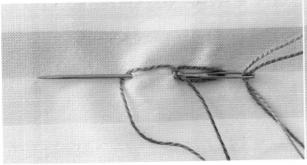

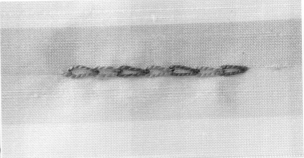

3. Take a stitch to the back of the fabric where the thread emerged from the last stitch, using the same hole and sliding the needle under the fabric. Loop the second color of thread *under* the needle, and repeat Step 2.

4. Continue as needed. To finish the stitch, take the needle to the back of the fabric just on the other side of the thread that formed the last loop.

Chevron Stitch

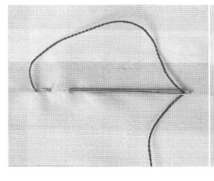 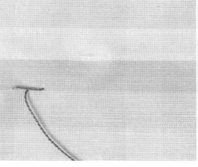 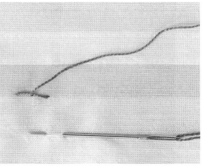

1. Bring up the needle on the edge of a stripe or crazy quilt seam, and move the needle to the right. Take a stitch to the left that is half the length of the stitch.

2. Pull the thread to the front of the fabric, making sure the thread is centered below the stitch.

3. Move the needle to the right and down to the lower edge of the stripe or seam. Take a stitch to the left.

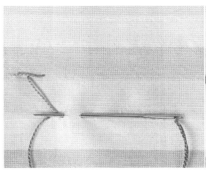 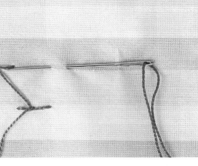 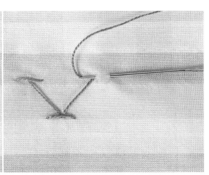

4. Pull the needle to the front of the fabric, and move the needle to the right. Take a stitch back to the left, making sure the stitch is close to the thread in the center.

5. Pull the thread to the front of the fabric, making sure the thread is centered and above the stripe or seam. Move the needle to the right and up to the top edge of the stripe or seam. Take a stitch to the right.

6. Pull the needle to the front of the fabric, and move the needle to the right, staying on the top edge of the stripe or seam. Take a stitch back to the left, making sure the stitch is close to the thread in the center.

7. Continue as needed.

Chevron Stitch—Beaded

For this stitch, use a needle with an eye big enough for the thread but small enough to go through the hole of the bead. An embroidery needle usually works well for this purpose. Refer to Chevron Stitch (page 29) as needed.

  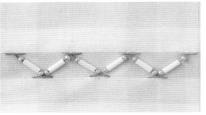

1. Follow Chevron Stitch, Steps 1 and 2. String your chosen beads on the thread.

2. Take a stitch to the right, following Chevron Stitch, Steps 3 and 4. String your chosen beads on the thread.

3. Repeat Steps 1 and 2 as needed.

Couching Stitch

A Couching Stitch is used to tack down a long Straight Stitch (page 46). For demonstrational purposes, I used a contrasting color of thread. If you want the couching to blend in, use the same thread you used for the Straight Stitch. It is best to couch long Straight Stitches every ¼″–⅜″.

Bring the needle to the front of the fabric on one side of the thread, and take the needle to the back of the fabric on the other side of the thread.

> **TIP**
>
> The Couching Stitch will look better if you don't use the same hole that you came up from the fabric to go back down. Instead, take the thread to the back of the fabric just a thread's width away. Think of these Couching Stitches as small Straight Stitches or staples holding down the long Straight Stitch.

Cretan Stitch

To get a good feel for this stitch, stitch it two stripe widths, as demonstrated, rather than one stripe width.

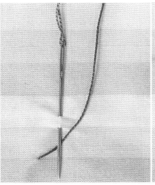 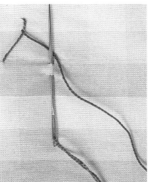 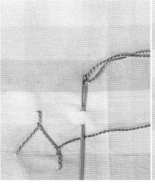 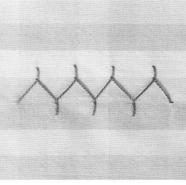

1. Bring up the needle on the middle line of the 2 stripes. (*Note:* If you are stitching on a crazy quilt seam, bring up the needle on the seam.) Move the needle to the right, and take a ¼″ stitch above the top stripe line. Make sure the thread is *under* the needle.

2. Move the needle to the right, and take a ¼″ stitch below the bottom stripe, making sure the thread is *under* the needle.

3. Move the needle to the right, and take a ¼″ stitch above the top stripe, making sure the thread is *under* the needle.

4. Continue as needed.

Cretan Stitch—Beaded 1

For this stitch, use a needle with an eye big enough for the thread but small enough to go through the hole of the bead. An embroidery needle usually works well for this purpose. Refer to Cretan Stitch (above) as needed.

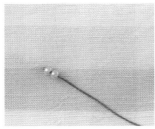 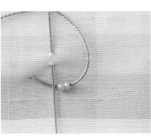 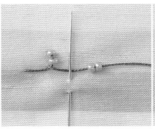 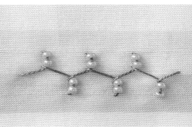

1. Pull the thread to the front of the fabric, and string 2 beads on it.

2. Follow Cretan Stitch, Step 1, keeping the 2 beads to the *right* of the needle.

3. String 2 more beads on the thread, and follow Cretan Stitch, Step 2, keeping the 2 beads to the *right* of the needle.

4. Continue as needed.

Cretan Stitch—Beaded 2

For this stitch, use a needle with an eye big enough for the thread but small enough to go through the hole of the bead. An embroidery needle usually works well for this purpose. Refer to Cretan Stitch (page 31) as needed.

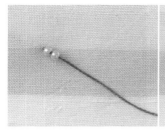 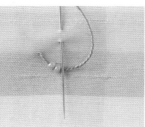 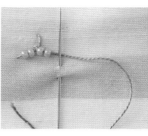 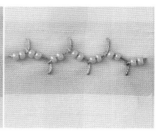

1. Pull the thread to the front of the fabric, and string 2 beads on it.

2. Follow Cretan Stitch, Step 1, keeping the 2 beads to the *left* of the needle.

3. String 2 more beads on the thread, and follow Cretan Stitch, Step 2, keeping the 2 beads to the *left* of the needle.

4. Continue as needed.

Cretan Stitch—Beaded 3

For this stitch, use a needle with an eye big enough for the thread but small enough to go through the hole of the bead. An embroidery needle usually works well for this purpose. You may use one color of bead or add interest by using two colors of beads. Refer to Cretan Stitch (page 31) as needed.

 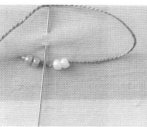  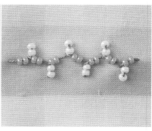

1. Pull the thread to the front of the fabric, and string 4 beads on it.

2. Follow Cretan Stitch, Step 1, keeping 2 beads on either side of the needle.

3. String 4 more beads on the thread, and follow Cretan Stitch, Step 2.

4. Continue as needed.

Cretan/Blanket Combination Stitch

See Blanket/Cretan Combination Stitch (page 21).

Cretan/Herringbone Combination Stitch

See Herringbone/Cretan Combination Stitch (page 41).

Cross Stitch

Cross Stitch is done by stitching one row of half-stitches going at a diagonal to the right and then moving back toward the left to do the second half of the stitch at a diagonal to the left.

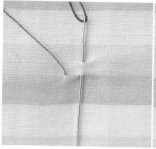 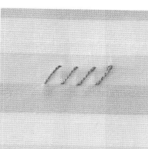 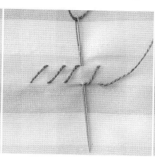 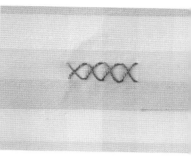

1. Bring the needle to the front of the fabric on the lower edge of the stripe or crazy quilt seam. Take a stitch at a 45° angle to the right, taking the needle to the back of the fabric. In the same movement, bring the needle back to the front of the fabric on the lower edge of the stripe or seam.

2. Repeat Step 1 as many times as needed, moving to the right.

3. Bring the needle to the front of the fabric on the lower edge of the stripe or seam, as shown. Take a stitch at a 45° angle to the left, using the same hole that was created from the previous stitch and taking the needle to the back of the fabric. In the same movement, bring the needle to the front of the fabric on the lower edge of the stripe or seam, using the same hole from the previous stitch.

4. Continue as needed.

Detached Wheatear Stitch

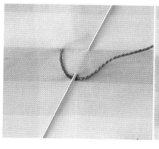 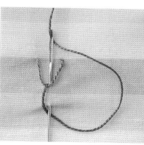 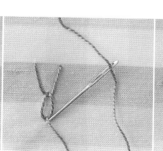 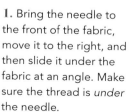

1. Bring the needle to the front of the fabric, move it to the right, and then slide it under the fabric at an angle. Make sure the thread is *under* the needle.

2. Pull the thread to the front of the fabric, and take a stitch to the back, using the same hole where the thread emerged. Slide the needle under the fabric, and bring it to the front of the fabric below the previous stitch. Make sure the thread is *under* the needle.

3. Take the thread to the back of the fabric, stitching just on the other side of the thread that forms the loop.

Feather Stitch

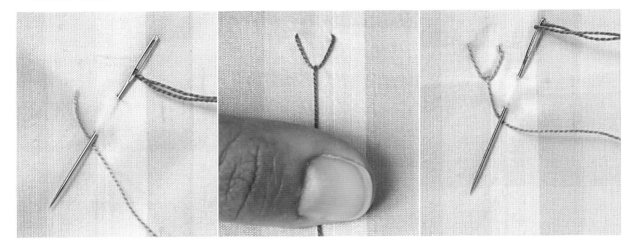

1. Bring up the needle on the left side of the stripe or crazy quilt seam. Move the needle to the right, and then slide the needle under the fabric at an angle. Make sure the thread is *under* the needle, as shown.

TIP
By varying the angle of the needle, you can make the Feather Stitch look completely different. Experiment with the angles, and see how many different Feather Stitches you can make.

2. Pull the needle out from the fabric, and gently pull the thread up and then down. Hold it in place with your left thumb.

3. Move the needle to the right, and repeat Step 1.

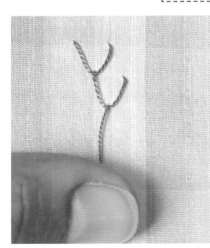
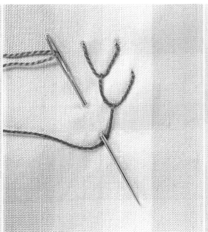

4. Pull the needle out from the fabric, and gently pull the thread up and then down, as you did in Step 2.

5. Move the needle to the left, and repeat Step 1.

6. Continue as needed.

Feather Stitch—Double

This stitch is very similar to a basic Feather Stitch. The only difference is the direction in which you move the needle and thread.

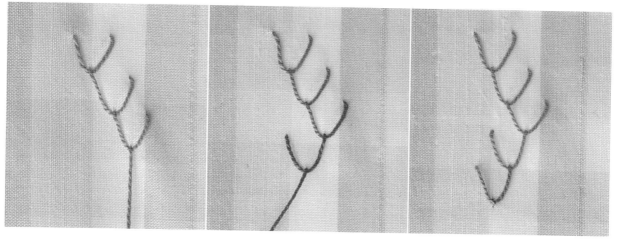

1. Follow Feather Stitch, Steps 1–4 (previous page).

2. Move the needle to the right, and repeat Feather Stitch, Step 1.

3. Move the needle to the left, and repeat Feather Stitch, Step 1. Repeat this step again, moving the needle to the left.

4. Continue as needed.

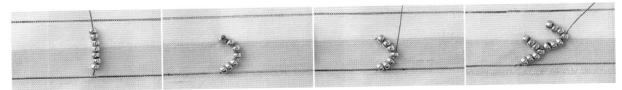

Feather Stitch—Double, Beaded

For demonstrational purposes, I used red beading thread to make it easier to see the stitch. Normally I use a thread that matches either the fabric or the bead, depending on the project. Also for demonstrational purposes, I used a pen to mark my lines; normally I use a purple air-erasable pen that fades away after I finish stitching.

1. Draw a ¼″ line on either side of the striped fabric or crazy quilt seam. Bring the needle and thread to the front of the fabric on the lower edge of the drawn line, and string 7 beads on the thread.

2. Take the needle to the back of the fabric on the stripe or seamline.

3. Bring the needle and thread to the front of the fabric, coming up close to where the middle (fourth) bead on the string sits when it lies flat on the fabric. Move the needle in an *upward* direction, and slide it through the middle bead. Pull the needle out of the middle bead, and string 7 more beads on the thread.

4. Take the needle and thread to the back of the fabric, halfway between the stripe or seamline and the upper drawn line. Repeat Step 3.

5. Take the needle and thread to the back of the fabric on the edge of the upper line. Bring the needle and thread to the front of the fabric, coming up close to where the middle bead on the string sits when it lies flat on the fabric. Move the needle in a *downward* direction, and slide it through the middle bead. Pull the needle out of the middle bead, and string 7 more beads on the thread.

6. Take the needle to the back of the fabric, halfway between the stripe or seamline and the lower drawn line. Bring the needle and thread to the front of the fabric, coming up close to where the middle bead on the string sits when it lies flat on the fabric. Move the needle in a *downward* direction, and slide it through the middle bead. Pull the needle out of the middle bead, and string 7 more beads on the thread.

7. Take the needle and thread to the back of the fabric on the edge of the lower stripe. To finish the stitch, bring the needle and thread to the front of the fabric, coming up close to where the middle bead on the string sits when it lies flat on the fabric. Move the needle in an *upward* direction, and slide it through the middle bead. Pull the needle out of the middle bead, and take the needle to the back of the fabric on the other side of the bead. To continue the stitch, string 7 beads on the thread and repeat Steps 4–7 as needed.

Feather Stitch—Triple

This stitch is very similar to a basic Feather Stitch. The only difference is the direction that you move the needle and thread.

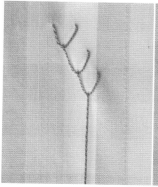   

1. Follow Feather Stitch, Steps 1–4 (page 34).

2. Move the needle to the right, and repeat Feather Stitch, Step 1.

3. Move the needle to the right again. Repeat Feather Stitch, Step 1.

4. Move the needle to the left, and repeat Feather Stitch, Step 1. Repeat this step 2 more times, moving the needle to the left.

5. Continue as needed.

Feather Stitch—Knotted

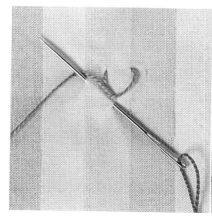 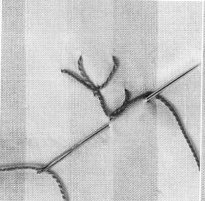 

1. Follow Feather Stitch, Steps 1 and 2 (page 34), and then take a stitch that starts at the base of the Feather Stitch and angles outward. Loop the thread around the needle, as shown, and pull the needle toward you until the stitch lies flat on the fabric.

2. Follow Feather Stitch, Steps 3 and 4; then repeat Step 1 (at left), looping the thread around the needle as shown.

3. Continue as needed.

Fly Stitch

This stitch is also called the Y-Stitch.

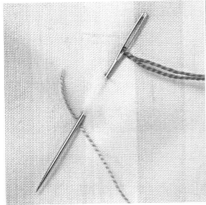
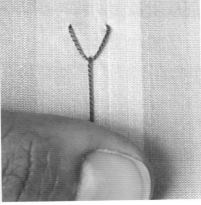
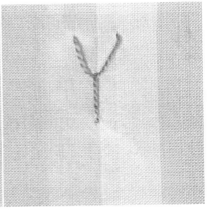

1. Bring up the needle to the left of the stripe or crazy quilt seam. Move the needle to the right, and then slide it under the fabric at an angle. Make sure the thread is *under* the needle, as shown.

2. Pull the needle out from the fabric, and gently pull the thread up and then down. Hold it in place with your left thumb.

3. Take the thread to the back of the fabric.

- -

Fly Stitch—Beaded

For demonstrational purposes, I used red beading thread to make it easier to see the stitch. Normally I use a thread that matches either the fabric or the bead, depending on the project.

1. Bring up the needle on the edge of a stripe or crazy quilt seam, and string 6 beads on the thread.

2. Move the needle ¼˝ to the right, and take it to the back of the fabric.

3. Bring up the needle just inside the loop that was formed in Step 2, with 3 beads on each side, making sure that a V is formed and the beads lie flat on the fabric.

4. String 4 beads on the thread.

5. Take the needle to the back of the fabric, making sure the beads lie flat on the fabric.

Fly Stitch / Bullion Knot Combination Stitch

See Bullion Knot/Fly Stitch Combination Stitch (page 23).

French Knot

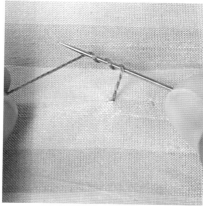 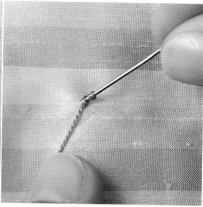 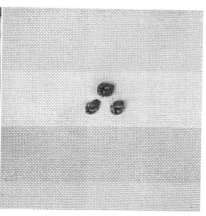

1. Bring the needle to the front of the fabric. Holding the needle in your right hand, take the thread in your left hand and bring it in front of the needle. Wrap the thread twice around the needle.

2. Take the needle to the back of the fabric close to where you came up, holding the thread in your left hand. Pull the thread until the French Knot is snug against the fabric.

Herringbone Stitch

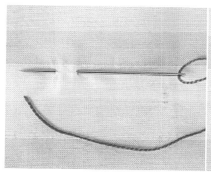 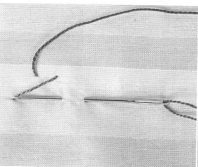 

1. Bring up the needle on the lower edge of the striped fabric or crazy quilt seam. Move the needle to the right, and take a stitch on the upper edge of the stripe or seam. Make sure the thread is placed below the needle.

2. Pull the thread out from the fabric. Move the needle to the right, and take a stitch on the lower edge of the stripe or seam in the same manner as before. Make sure the thread is placed above the needle.

3. Continue as needed.

Herringbone Stitch—Back Stitched

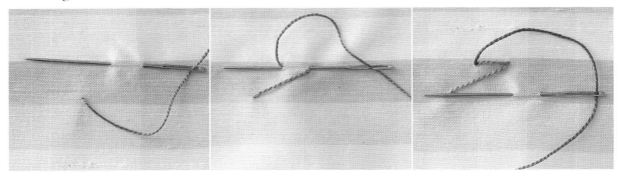

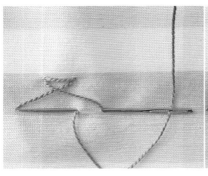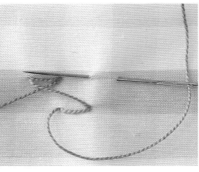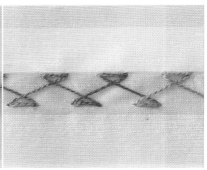

1. Bring up the needle on the lower edge of the striped fabric or crazy quilt seam. Move the needle to the right, and take a stitch on the upper edge of the stripe or seam. Make sure the thread is placed below the needle.

2. Pull the thread to the front of the fabric, and move the needle back to the right. Take a stitch going into the same hole where the thread went to the back of the fabric. Slide the needle under the fabric, moving to the left, and reemerge in the same hole where the thread came out of the fabric. Make sure to keep the thread placed above the needle while doing this part of the stitch.

3. Pull the thread out from the fabric. Move the needle to the right, and take a stitch on the lower edge of the stripe or seam in the same manner as before. Make sure that the thread is placed above the needle.

4. Pull the thread to the front of the fabric, and move the needle back to the right. Take a stitch going into the same hole where the thread went to the back of the fabric. Slide the needle under the fabric, moving to the left, and reemerge in the same hole where the thread came out of the fabric. Make sure to keep the thread placed below the needle while doing this part of the stitch.

5. Pull the needle to the front of the fabric, and repeat Step 2.

6. Continue as needed.

Herringbone/Blanket Combination Stitch

Refer to Herringbone Stitch (page 39) and Blanket Stitch (page 16) as needed.

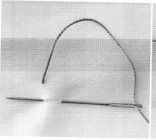 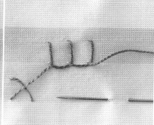 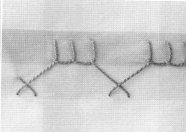

1. Bring the needle to the front of the fabric in the middle of the lower stripe. Move the needle to the right, and take a stitch back to the left on the lower edge of the stripe. The needle should reemerge directly below where the thread came out of the fabric. Make sure the thread is placed above the needle. Pull the needle to the front of the fabric.

2. Move the needle to the right, and place the needle in a perpendicular position, moving in a downward direction. Make sure the thread is placed *under* the needle.

3. Repeat Step 2 twice. Move the needle to the right, and take a stitch back to the left on the lower edge of the stripe. Make sure the thread is placed above the needle. Pull the needle to the front of the fabric.

4. Repeat Steps 2 and 3 as needed.

Herringbone/Cretan Combination Stitch

Refer to Herringbone Stitch (page 39) and Cretan Stitch (page 31) as needed.

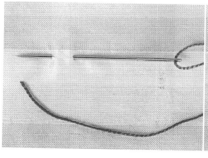 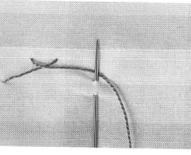 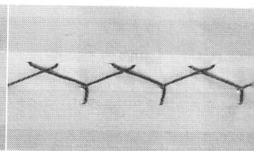

1. Bring up the needle on the lower edge of the striped fabric or crazy quilt seam. Move the needle to the right, and take a stitch that is parallel to the upper edge of the stripe or seam and that moves from right to left. Make sure the thread is placed below the needle.

2. Move the needle to the right, and take a stitch below the lower edge of the stripe or seam, making sure the thread is *under* the needle.

3. Move the needle to the right, and repeat Step 1.

4. Continue as needed.

Lazy Daisy

This stitch is also called the Detached Chain Stitch.

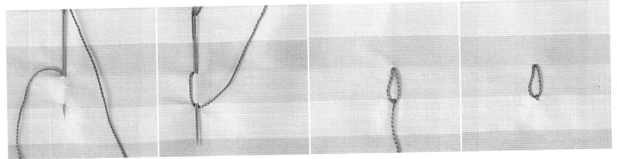

1. Pull the thread to the front of the fabric on the edge of the stripe or seam. Take a stitch to the back of the fabric using the same hole where the thread emerged from the fabric. Slide the needle under the fabric and bring it to the front of the fabric below the previous stitch. Make sure the thread is *under* the needle.

2. Pull the thread to the front of the fabric.

3. Pull on the thread until the stitch forms a loop. You can control the shape of this loop by the amount of tension you have on the thread.

4. Take the thread to the back of the fabric, stitching just on the other side of the thread that forms the loop.

Lazy Daisy / Bullion Knot Combination Stitch

See Bullion Knot/Lazy Daisy Combination Stitch (page 24).

Pistil Stitch

This stitch incorporates a French Knot. Refer to French Knot (page 39) as needed.

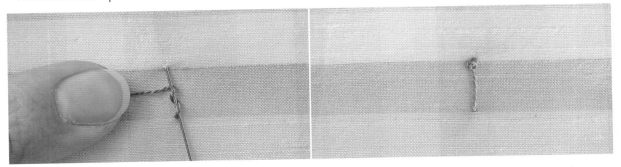

Pull the thread to the front of the fabric. Wrap the thread around the needle twice, and take it to the back of the fabric ⅜″ from where the thread emerged from the fabric. While holding the thread with your left thumb, pull the thread until the French Knot is snug against the fabric.

Rosette Stitch

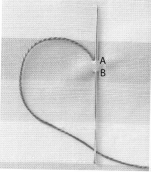 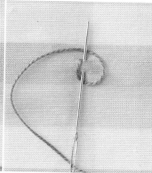 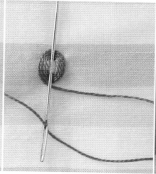 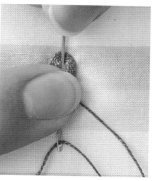

1. Pull the needle and thread to the front of the fabric at A. Take a stitch about ¼″ to B, and push the tip of the needle to come out at A again, making sure not to pull the needle through the fabric.

2. Wrap the thread around the needle in a counterclockwise direction under the needle.

3. Wrap the thread around the needle 4 times, and end with the thread on the right side of the needle on the lower end of the stitch.

4. Hold the wraps with your left thumb, and pull the needle through the wraps with your right hand.

5. Take the needle to the back of the fabric just on the other side of the outside edge of the wraps. *Make sure not to pull too tightly—you want to leave the loop that has formed on the bottom of the wraps in place.*

6. Bring up the needle through the inside of the loops on the bottom of the wraps. Take the needle to the back of the fabric on the other side of the loops.

Running Stitch

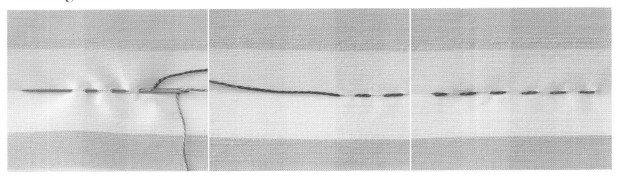

1. Pull the thread to the front of the fabric, and move the needle in and out of the fabric at equal distances.

2. Pull the thread to the front of the fabric, and repeat Step 1 as needed.

Sheaf Stitch

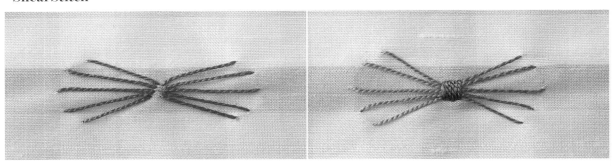

1. Pull the needle and thread to the front of the fabric, and make a series of angled horizontal Straight Stitches, as shown.

2. Make a series of vertical Straight Stitches close together to fill in the space between the 2 sets of horizontal Straight Stitches.

Star Stitch

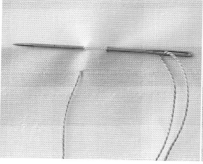 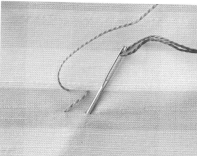 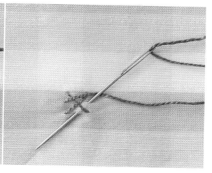

1. Bring the needle to the front of the fabric, and take a stitch at a 45° angle to the right, taking the needle to the back of the fabric. In the same movement, going to the left, bring the needle back to the front of the fabric on the top edge of the stripe or crazy quilt seam.

2. Pull the needle to the front of the fabric, and take a stitch at a 45° angle to the right, taking the needle to the back of the fabric.

3. Bring the needle to the front of the fabric on the left side of the stitch, and take a stitch to the right, taking the needle to the back of the fabric. In the same movement, angle the needle to the lower edge of the stitch, bringing the needle to the front of the fabric.

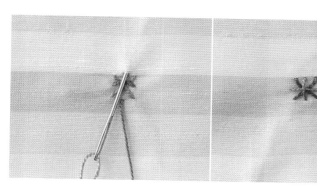

4. Pull the needle to the front of the fabric, and take a stitch on the top edge of the stripe or seam, as shown. Take the needle to the back of the fabric.

Stem Stitch

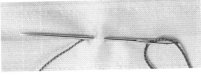  

1. Bring up the needle on the edge of the stripe or crazy quilt seam. Move the needle to the right, and take a stitch to the left, making sure to keep the thread placed below the needle.

2. Pull the needle to the front of the fabric, and move the needle to the right. Take a stitch to the left, keeping the thread placed below the needle, and come up close to the last stitch that you made.

3. Repeat Step 2 as needed.

Stem Stitch—Beaded

For demonstrational purposes, I used red beading thread to make it easier to see the stitch. Normally I use a thread that matches either the fabric or the bead, depending on the project.

1. Bring up the needle on the edge of the stripe or crazy quilt seam, and string 6 beads on the thread.

2. Take the needle to the back of the fabric, making sure the beads lie flat on the fabric. Bring the needle back up on the edge of the same stripe or seam, counting back 2 beads.

3. String 6 more beads on the thread, and repeat Step 2.

4. Continue as needed. To give the stitch a more finished look, add 2 beads on the end of the upper right side and 2 beads on the end of the lower left side.

Straight Stitch

 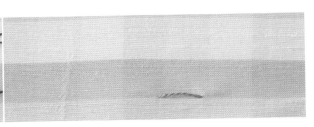

1. Pull the needle to the front of the fabric, and move the needle over the distance needed to complete the stitch.

2. Take the stitch to the back of the fabric.

silk ribbon embroidery stitches

THREADING AND KNOTTING SILK RIBBON

Embroidering with silk ribbon is a little bit different than with thread. One big difference is the way you thread the needle and tie the knot on the end. For silk ribbon embroidery, it is best to use a #22 or #24 chenille needle. You may use silk ribbon to do regular embroidery stitches, but keep in mind that you should use less tension when pulling on the stitch so that the ribbon will look soft and full.

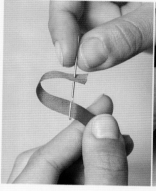 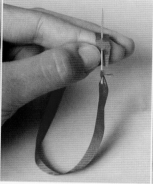 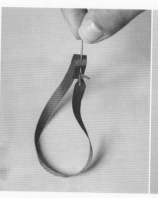 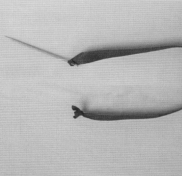

1. Thread the silk ribbon through the eye of the needle. Pierce the end of the ribbon with the needle about ¼" from the raw edge.

2. To knot the end of the ribbon, grab the lower raw edge between your thumb and forefinger. Wrap the ribbon away from you around your forefinger. Take a stitch through the ribbon on your finger about ¼" from the raw edge.

3. Pull the ribbon down over the eye of the needle and continue moving it down the length of the ribbon until a knot forms.

Silk ribbon after being threaded and knotted correctly

Chain-Stitch Rose

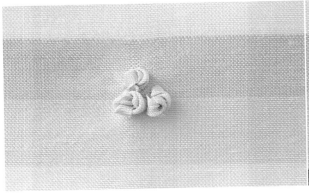

1. Embroider 3 French Knots (page 39) with silk ribbon to make a center for the rose.

2. Bring the needle to the front of the fabric, close to the 3 French Knots. Stitch a Chain Stitch (page 25) in silk ribbon, working in a counterclockwise direction around the center French Knots. Continue to Chain Stitch, spiraling out until the rose is the desired size.

3. Take the needle to the back of the fabric, just on the other side of the ribbon that formed the last loop.

Colonial Knot

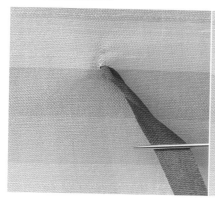

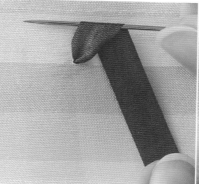

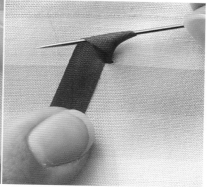

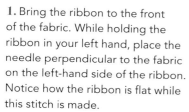

1. Bring the ribbon to the front of the fabric. While holding the ribbon in your left hand, place the needle perpendicular to the fabric on the left-hand side of the ribbon. Notice how the ribbon is flat while this stitch is made.

2. While holding the needle in the perpendicular position and still holding the ribbon in your left hand, rotate the needle in a counterclockwise motion until the needle is in a horizontal position, as shown.

3. Wrap the ribbon that is in your left hand around the needle once, moving from the top to the bottom. *Keep the tension in the ribbon loose to make a softer-looking Colonial Knot.*

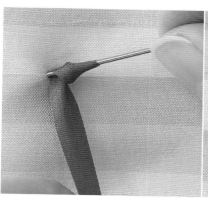

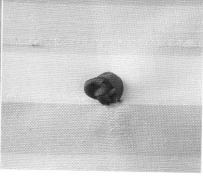

4. Take the ribbon to the back of the fabric, close to where the ribbon came up, without catching the knot on the back of the fabric. *Make sure not to pull too tightly, or the Colonial Knot will become very small.*

Colonial Knot Running Stitch Rose

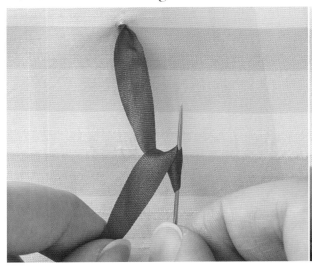

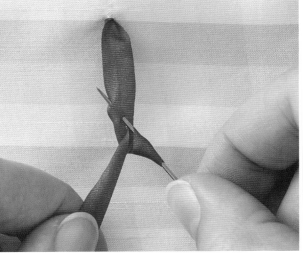

1. Pull the ribbon to the front of the fabric. Follow Colonial Knot, Steps 1–3 (page 49) using silk ribbon, leaving 1½˝ of ribbon between the fabric and the in-progress Colonial Knot.

2. Make a Running Stitch along the length of the ribbon left between the fabric and the Colonial Knot, moving the needle back and forth in a zigzag motion from the left edge to the right edge of the ribbon. This will make the rose look fuller.

> **TIP**
> The smaller you make the Running Stitch, the smaller the rose will be, and vice versa.

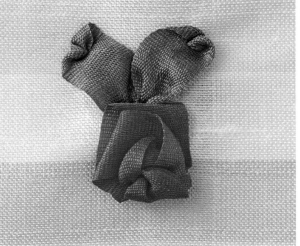

3. After completing the Running Stitch along the length of the ribbon, take the needle to the back of the fabric. *Make sure not to pull too tightly, or the rose won't look as full and natural.*

Loop Flower

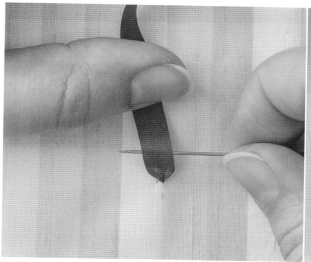

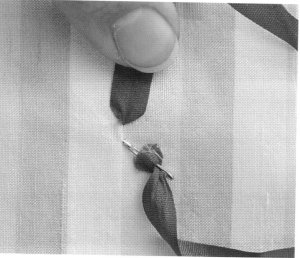

1. Bring the needle to the front of the fabric. Place the needle under the ribbon, and with slight pressure, move it toward the fabric. This helps smooth out any wrinkles in the ribbon.

2. Take the needle to the back of the fabric, just below the first stitch.

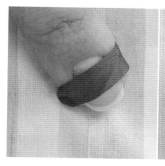

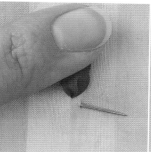

3. Pull the ribbon to the back of the fabric, keeping your index finger in the ribbon until the loop is the desired size.

4. Working in a clockwise direction, repeat Steps 1–3 to make a flower. *Make sure to pull gently, or the already stitched loops will pull through and will need to be stitched again.*

5. Make a French Knot (page 39) in silk ribbon in the center.

Plume Stitch

1. Follow Loop Flower, Steps 1–3 (page 51).

2. Hold the loop in place, and pierce the lower edge of the previous stitch before bringing the needle to the front of the fabric.

3. Take the needle to the back of the fabric, just below the last stitch. While pulling, keep your index finger in the ribbon until the loop is the desired size, as in Loop Flower, Step 3.

4. Repeat Steps 2 and 3 to complete the desired number of loops. Pull the last loop flat.

Ribbon Stitch

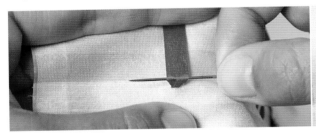 

1. Bring the needle to the front of the fabric. Place the needle under the ribbon, and with slight pressure, move it toward the fabric. This helps smooth out any wrinkles in the ribbon.

2. Pierce the middle of the ribbon with the needle about ½˝ from where it came out of the fabric. Pierce into the fabric as well.

> **TIP**
> You may make this stitch any length to fit the project you are working on. To give the stitch a more natural look, ease some of the tension in the ribbon before piercing it with the needle.

3. Pull the needle to the back of the fabric until the ribbon comes to a point. Repeat Steps 1–3 to make a flower and leaves. Make a French Knot (page 39) in silk ribbon in the center.

Side Ribbon Stitch Flower

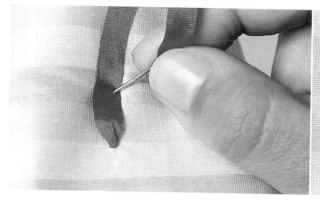

1. Follow Ribbon Stitch, Step 1 (previous page).

2. Pierce the right edge of the ribbon with the needle.

3. Gently pull the needle to the back of the fabric until the ribbon comes to a point.

4. Bring the ribbon up on the right side of the first stitch you made. Pierce the *left* edge of the ribbon with the needle. Gently pull the needle to the back of the fabric until the ribbon comes to a point. Repeat Steps 1–3 to make a flower and leaves. Make a French Knot (page 39) in the center.

Spider Web Rose

For demonstrational purposes, I used a pen to mark my circle; normally I use a purple air-erasable pen that fades away after I finish stitching.

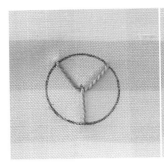   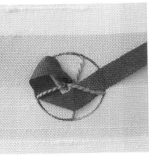

1. Draw a circle on the fabric and mark the center. Stitch a Fly Stitch (page 38) in thread, using the center mark as a guide.

2. Stitch 2 Straight Stitches (page 46) in thread on either side of the Fly Stitch, taking the needle from the outside line and going to the back of the fabric in the center of the circle for each stitch. Make sure the stitches are evenly placed around the circle. You should end up with 5 spokes as a foundation for the rose.

3. Switching to a needle that has been threaded with silk ribbon, bring the needle to the front of the fabric, very close to the center.

4. In a counterclockwise direction, weave the ribbon over and under the spokes to complete the first round.

 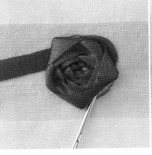 

5. After completing the first round, pull the ribbon snug against the center threads so they won't show.

6. Continue in a counterclockwise direction, weaving the ribbon over and under the spokes until the threads are no longer visible. Use less tension on the ribbon to give the rose some fullness. Take the ribbon to the back of the fabric just under the ribbon.

Stem Stitch Rose

1. Embroider 3 French Knots (page 39) with silk ribbon to make a center for the rose.

2. Bring the needle to the front of the fabric close to the 3 French Knots. Stitch a Stem Stitch (page 46) in silk ribbon, working in a counterclockwise direction near the center French Knots. Continue to make Stem Stitches, spiraling out until the rose is the desired size.

3. Take the ribbon to the back of the fabric just under the ribbon.

Straight-Stitch Flower

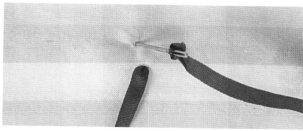 

Bring the needle to the front of the fabric, and take a stitch ¼˝ away, leaving the ribbon loose. Repeat to make a flower and leaves. Make a French Knot (page 39) in the center.

Combination Stitches

This chapter contains 500 different stitch combinations that I used while working on my crazy quilt. I loved the challenge of finding new ways to use the same embroidery stitches I already knew. I hope that looking through this chapter will inspire you to find new and different ways to combine stitches. By changing the colors of the thread or trying the stitch with ribbon floss or silk ribbon, you can make the stitch look completely different.

Adding beads, buttons, and rose montées are other good ways to change the look of the stitch.

The instructions under each photo are written in the stitching order that I used. So if a caption lists Back Stitch first, that is what I did first. Some stitches are organized by motif or design elements, but most are organized by the first stitch I used in the combination.

I hope that you are inspired by all of the combinations and enjoy doing them as you stitch every day!

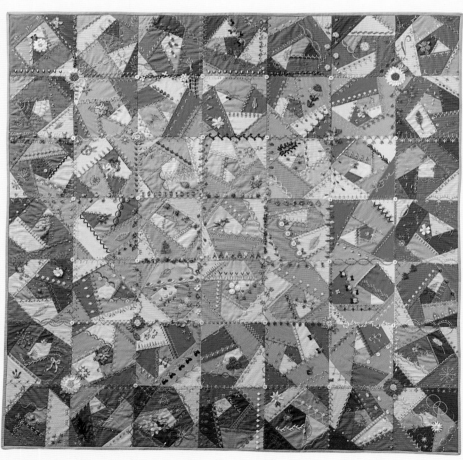

Joyful Embellishments, 41″ × 41″, by Valerie Bothell, 2017

back stitch combinations

Back Stitch + Glass Flower Beads + Seed Beads

Back Stitch + Lazy Daisy + Glass Flower Beads + Seed Beads

Back Stitch + Straight Stitch + Pearls

Back Stitch + Lazy Daisy + Seed Beads

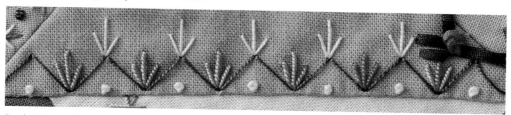

Back Stitch + Straight Stitch + French Knot

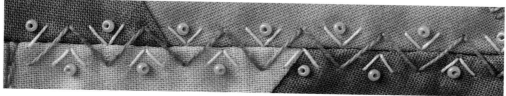

Back Stitch + Straight Stitch + Seed Beads

Back Stitch (3 colors)

Back Stitch + Straight Stitch + French Knot

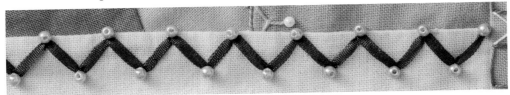

Back Stitch (2mm silk ribbon) + Pearls

Back Stitch (2mm silk ribbon) + Colonial Knot Running Stitch Rose (4mm silk ribbon) + Lazy Daisy leaves

Back Stitch (2 different colors) + Pearls

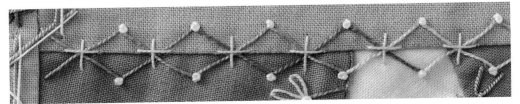

Back Stitch (twice) + French Knot + Cross Stitch

Back Stitch (twice) + Cross Stitch + Lazy Daisy + Seed Beads

Back Stitch + Seed Beads

Back Stitch + French Knot

Back Stitch + Straight Stitch

Back Stitch + Straight Stitch

Back Stitch + Cross Stitch + Lazy Daisy

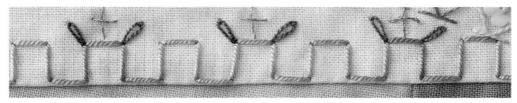

Back Stitch + Cross Stitch + Lazy Daisy

Back Stitch + Lazy Daisy + French Knot

Back Stitch + Loop Flower (4 mm silk ribbon) + French Knot (4 mm silk ribbon)

Back Stitch + French Knot

Back Stitch + Pearls

Back Stitch + Lazy Daisy + Pearls + Seed Beads

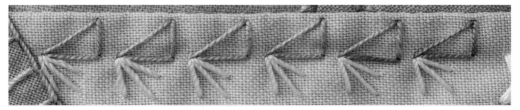

Back Stitch + Straight Stitch

Back Stitch + French Knot

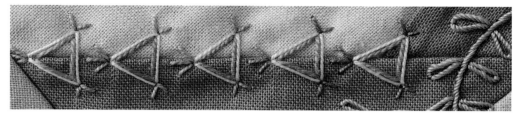

Back Stitch (2 different colors) + Straight Stitch

Back Stitch (3 different colors)

Back Stitch + Straight Stitch + French Knot

Back Stitch + Straight Stitch + French Knot

Back Stitch + Straight Stitch + Lazy Daisy leaves + French Knot + Sequin Flowers + Seed Beads

Back Stitch + Cross Stitch + Pearls

Back Stitch + Straight Stitch + Seed Bead

Back Stitch + Seed Beads + Bugle Beads

Back Stitch + Lazy Daisy + French Knot

Back Stitch + Lazy Daisy + Pearls

Back Stitch + Cross Stitch + Star Stitch

Back Stitch + Star Stitch + French Knot

Back Stitch + French Knot

Back Stitch + Star Stitch

Back Stitch + Lazy Daisy +
Straight Stitch + French Knot +
Seed Beads

Back Stitch + Star Stitch + Lazy Daisy

Back Stitch + Star Stitch + French Knot

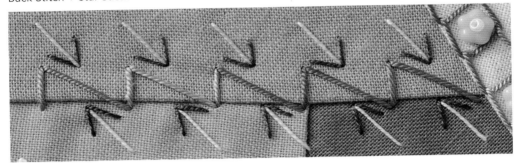

Back Stitch + Straight Stitch

Back Stitch

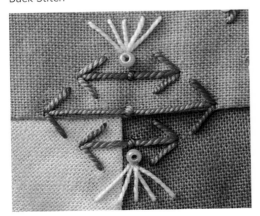

Back Stitch + Straight Stitch (Couched) +
Seed Beads

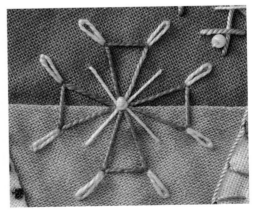

Back Stitch + Lazy Daisy + Cross Stitch +
French Knot

beaded stitch combinations

Rose Montée + Seed Beads + Oval Pearls

Seed Beads + Pearl

Seed Beads + Ribbon Stitch + Running Stitch

Seed Beads

Stem Stitch—Beaded (with Seed Beads)

Bugle Beads + Pearls + Lazy Daisy

Chevron Stitch—Beaded (with Seed Beads and Bugle Beads)

Blanket Stitch—Beaded 1 (with Pearls)

Seed Beads + Oval Pearls

Cretan Stitch—Beaded 2 (with Seed Beads)

Cretan Stitch—Beaded 1 (with Seed Beads) + Straight Stitch

Cretan Stitch—Beaded 3 (with Seed Beads)

Chain Stitch—Open, Beaded (with Seed Beads)

Feather Stitch—Double, Beaded (with Seed Beads)

Feather Stitch—Beaded leaf (with Seed Beads)

Fly Stitch—Beaded (with Seed Beads)

Fly Stitch—Beaded (with Seed Beads)

Blanket Stitch—Beaded 2 (with Pearls)

Blanket Stitch—Beaded 2 (with Seed Beads)

Rose Montées

Pearl + Seed Bead rose and leaves

blanket stitch combinations

Blanket Stitch + Fly Stitch + Seed Beads

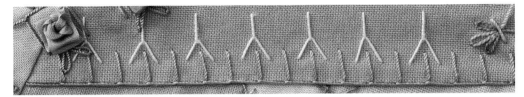

Blanket Stitch + Fly Stitch

Blanket Stitch + Lazy Daisy + Seed Beads

Blanket Stitch + Ribbon Stitch (4 mm silk ribbon)

Blanket Stitch + Rose Montée + Ribbon Stitch (4 mm silk ribbon)

Blanket Stitch + Colonial Knot Running Stitch Rose (7 mm silk ribbon) + Lazy Daisy

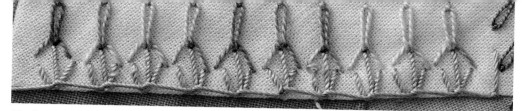

Blanket Stitch + Lazy Daisy + Straight Stitch

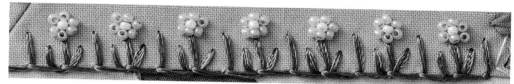

Blanket Stitch + Straight Stitch + Seed Bead flowers

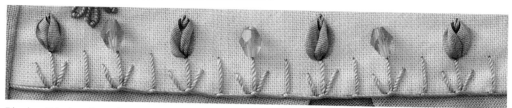

Blanket Stitch + Straight Stitch + Lazy Daisy (4mm silk ribbon) + Beads

Blanket Stitch + Lazy Daisy leaves + Lazy Daisy (4mm silk ribbon)

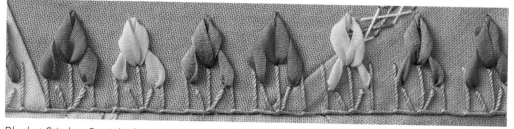

Blanket Stitch + Straight Stitch leaves + Lazy Daisy (4mm silk ribbon) + Straight Stitch (4mm silk ribbon)

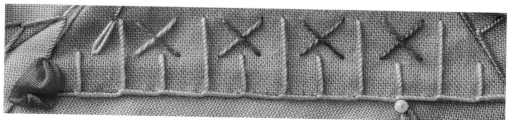

Blanket Stitch + Cross Stitch

Blanket Stitch + Lazy Daisy + Seed Beads

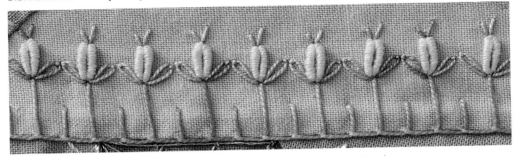

Blanket Stitch + Bullion Knot (2 side by side) + Lazy Daisy + Straight Stitch

Blanket Stitch + Lazy Daisy + Seed Beads

Blanket Stitch + Lazy Daisy

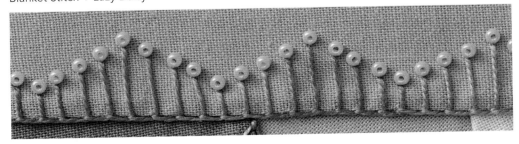

Blanket Stitch + Seed Beads

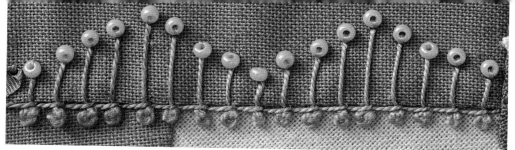

Blanket Stitch + Seed Beads + French Knot

Blanket Stitch + Lazy Daisy + Seed Beads

Blanket Stitch—Closed + Pearls

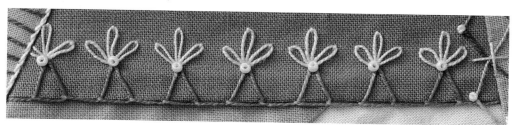

Blanket Stitch—Closed + Lazy Daisy + Seed Beads

Blanket Stitch—Closed + French Knot (7 mm silk ribbon) + Ribbon Stitch (7 mm silk ribbon)

Blanket Stitch + Straight Stitch

Blanket Stitch + Fly Stitch + French Knot + Lazy Daisy + Straight Stitch

Blanket Stitch + Lazy Daisy + French Knot

Blanket Stitch—Crossed + Sequin Flowers + Seed Beads

Blanket Stitch—Crossed + Lazy Daisy + French Knot

Blanket Stitch—Crossed

Blanket Stitch + Lazy Daisy

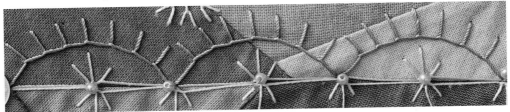

Blanket Stitch (3 times) + Pearls

Blanket Stitch + Colonial Knot Running Stitch Rose (7 mm silk ribbon) + Lazy Daisy leaves (2 mm silk ribbon) + Straight Stitch

Blanket Stitch + Colonial Knot Running Stitch Rose (7 mm silk ribbon) + Lazy Daisy leaves (2 mm silk ribbon)

Blanket Stitch + Pearls

Blanket Stitch + Seed Beads

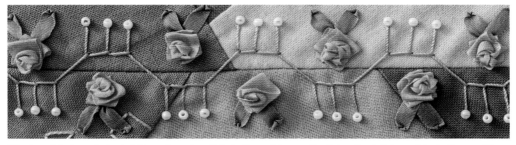

Blanket Stitch + Colonial Knot Running Stitch Rose (7 mm silk ribbon) + Ribbon Stitch (4 mm silk ribbon) + Seed Beads

Blanket Stitch + Seed Beads

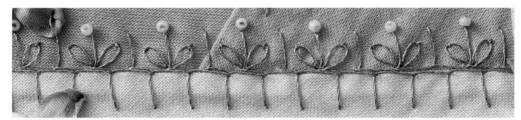

Blanket Stitch + Glass Flower Beads + Seed Beads

Blanket Stitch (each side of the seam) + Lazy Daisy + Seed Beads

Blanket Stitch—Knotted + Glass Flower Beads + Seed Beads

Blanket Stitch (twice)

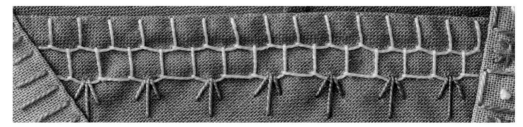

Blanket Stitch (twice) + Straight Stitch

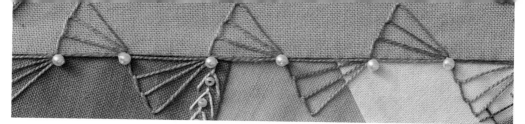

Blanket Stitch—Fan + Pearls

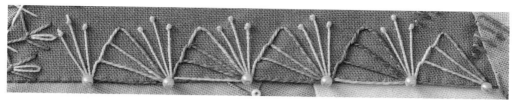

Blanket Stitch—Fan + Pistil Stitch + Pearls

Blanket Stitch—Fan + Pearls

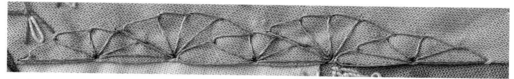

Blanket Stitch—Fan

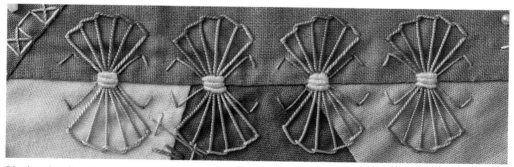

Blanket Stitch—Fan + Straight Stitch + Bullion Knot

Blanket Stitch—Circular

bullion knot combinations

Stem Stitch with Bullion Knot (3 different colors)

Bullion Knot

Bullion Knot + Pearls

Bullion Knot + Straight Stitch

Bullion Knot rose + Lazy Daisy

Bullion Knot rose + Straight Stitch + French Knot

Bullion Knot rose + Feather Stitch leaves

Bullion Knot rose + Lazy Daisy + French Knot

Bullion Knot rose + Stem Stitch + Lazy Daisy leaves + Straight Stitch + Seed Beads

Bullion Knot + Couched Fly Stitch

chain-stitch combinations

Chain Stitch + Back Stitch

Zigzag Chain Stitch + Seed Beads

Chain Stitch + French Knot

Chain Stitch + Lazy Daisy

Chain Stitch + French Knot + Lazy Daisy

Chain Stitch + Pistil Stitch + Pearls

Chain Stitch + Buttons + Ribbon Stitch (7 mm silk ribbon)

Chain Stitch + French Knot + Buttons

Chain Stitch + Straight Stitch + Seed Beads

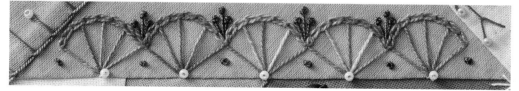

Chain Stitch + Straight Stitch + Pistil Stitch + French Knot + Seed Beads

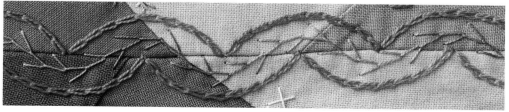

Chain Stitch + Feather Stitch

Chain Stitch + Colonial Knot Running Stitch Rose (7 mm silk ribbon) + Ribbon Stitch (7 mm silk ribbon)

Chain Stitch + Bugle Beads

Chain Stitch + Bugle Beads + Pearls

Chain Stitch + Feather Stitch

Chain Stitch + Feather Stitch + Lazy Daisy + Sequin Flowers + Seed Beads

Chain Stitch + Blanket Stitch + Seed Beads

Chain Stitch + Straight Stitch and Colonial Knot (7 mm silk ribbon) + Seed Beads

Chain Stitch + Colonial Knot Running Stitch Rose (7 mm silk ribbon) + Lazy Daisy (2 mm silk ribbon)

Chain Stitch (twice)

Chain Stitch (twice) + Straight Stitch + Star Stitch + Seed Beads

Chain Stitch (2 colors, twice)

Chain Stitch (3 times)

Chain Stitch + Straight Stitch + Seed Beads + Pearls

Chain Stitch—Open + Glass Flower Beads + Seed Beads

Chain Stitch—Feathered

Chain Stitch—Feathered + Back Stitch

Chain Stitch—Feathered (2 mm silk ribbon) + French Knot (4 mm silk ribbon)

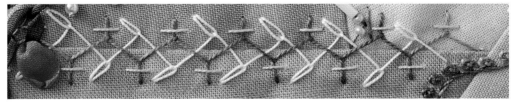

Chain Stitch—Feathered + Cretan Stitch + Straight Stitch

chevron stitch combinations

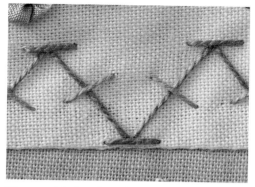

Chevron Stitch + Straight Stitch

Chevron Stitch + Lazy Daisy

Chevron Stitch + Lazy Daisy + Pearls

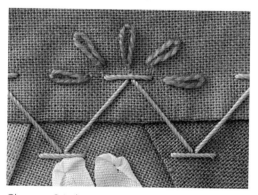

Chevron Stitch + Lazy Daisy

Chevron Stitch + Straight Stitch

Chevron Stitch + Straight Stitch + Pearls

Chevron Stitch + Lazy Daisy + Straight Stitch

Chevron Stitch + Lazy Daisy + French Knot + Straight Stitch

Chevron Stitch + Straight Stitch + Cross Stitch

Chevron Stitch + Lazy Daisy + Back Stitch

Chevron Stitch + Lazy Daisy + Cross Stitch + Oval Pearl

Chevron Stitch + Bugle Beads

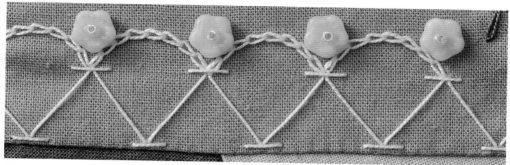

Chevron Stitch + Pearls + Sequins + Seed Beads

Chevron Stitch + Chain Stitch + Glass Flower Beads + Seed Beads

Chevron Stitch + Lazy Daisy + Glass Flower Beads + Seed Beads

Chevron Stitch + Straight Stitch + Glass Flower Beads + Seed Beads + Ribbon Stitch (7 mm silk ribbon)

Chevron Stitch + Straight Stitch + Lazy Daisy leaves + Lazy Daisy (4 mm silk ribbon)

Chevron Stitch + Lazy Daisy + French Knot + Ribbon Stitch (4 mm silk ribbon)

Chevron Stitch + Ribbon Stitch (7 mm silk ribbon) + French Knot (7 mm silk ribbon)

Chevron Stitch + Colonial Knot Running Stitch Rose (4 mm silk ribbon) + Ribbon Stitch (7 mm silk ribbon)

Chevron Stitch (twice) + Sequin Flowers + Seed Beads

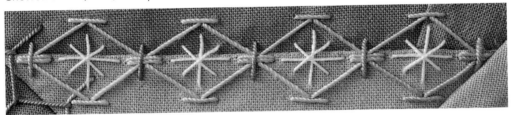

Chevron Stitch (twice) + Star Stitch + Straight Stitch

Chevron Stitch (twice) + Glass Flower Beads + Seed Beads

Slanted Chevron Stitch + Straight Stitch

Detached Chevron Stitch + Straight Stitch + French Knot

Chevron Stitch + Fly Stitch + Pearl

cretan stitch combinations

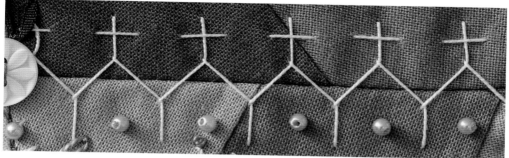

Cretan Stitch + Straight Stitch + Pearls

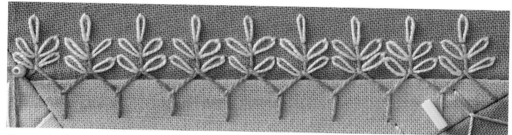

Cretan Stitch + Lazy Daisy

Cretan Stitch + Bullion Knot + Fly Stitch (2mm silk ribbon)

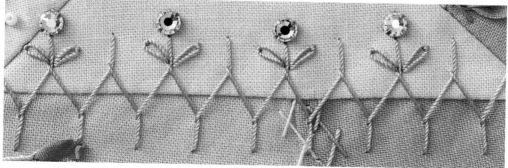

Cretan Stitch + Lazy Daisy + Rose Montées

Cretan Stitch + Lazy Daisy + Seed Beads

Cretan Stitch + Pearls + Ribbon Stitch (4 mm silk ribbon)

Cretan Stitch + Lazy Daisy leaves + Lazy Daisy (4 mm silk ribbon)

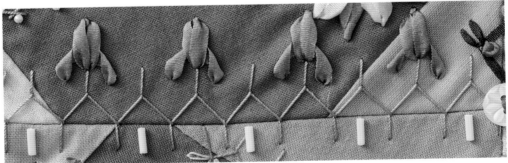

Cretan Stitch + Lazy Daisy (4 mm silk ribbon) + Straight Stitch (4 mm silk ribbon) + Bugle Beads

Cretan Stitch + Straight Stitch + Colonial Knot Running Stitch Rose (7 mm silk ribbon) + Lazy Daisy (2 mm silk ribbon)

Cretan Stitch + Cross Stitch + French Knot

Cretan Stitch + Straight Stitch + Star Stitch

Cretan Stitch + Cross Stitch + Pearls

Cretan Stitch + Lazy Daisy + Pearls

Cretan Stitch + Fly Stitch + Straight Stitch + Pearls

Cretan Stitch + Straight Stitch + Lazy Daisy + Seed Beads

Cretan Stitch + Lazy Daisy + Seed Beads + Pearls

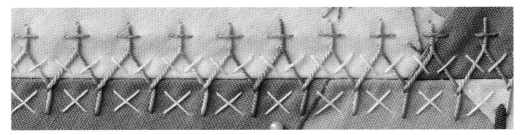

Cretan Stitch + Straight Stitch + Cross Stitch

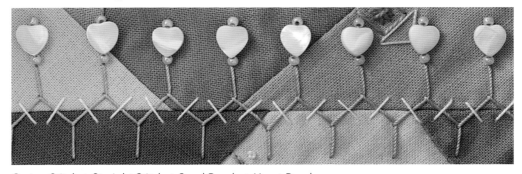

Cretan Stitch + Straight Stitch + Seed Beads + Heart Beads

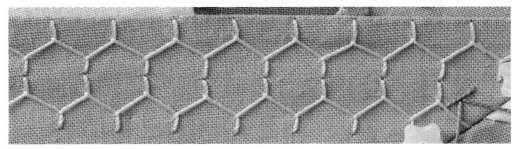

Cretan Stitch (twice)

Cretan Stitch (twice) + Seed Beads

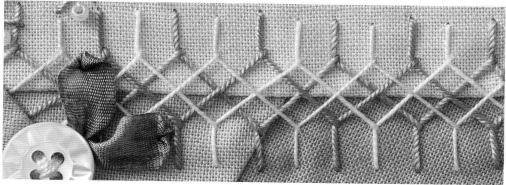

Cretan Stitch (4 times)

Cretan Stitch + Bugle Beads

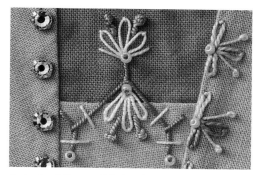

Detached Cretan Stitch + Lazy Daisy +
Straight Stitch + Pistil Stitch + Seed Beads

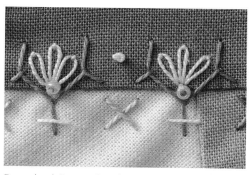

Detached Cretan Stitch + Cross Stitch +
Lazy Daisy + French Knot + Seed Beads

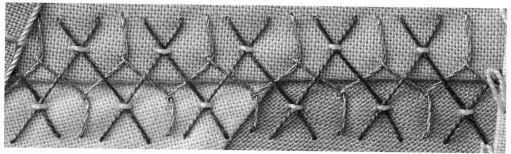

Cretan Stitch + Herringbone Stitch + Straight Stitch

cross-stitch combinations

Cross Stitch + Seed Beads

Cross Stitch + Lazy Daisy

Cross Stitch + Straight Stitch

Cross Stitch + Lazy Daisy + French Knot

Cross Stitch + Rose Montées

Cross Stitch + Straight Stitch

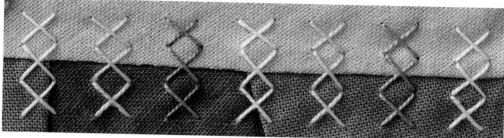

Stacked Cross Stitch

Cross Stitch + Straight Stitch + Pearls

Cross Stitch

Cross Stitch + Straight Stitch + Back Stitch

Cross Stitch + Straight Stitch + Back Stitch

Cross Stitch + Back Stitch + Straight Stitch + Seed Beads

Cross Stitch + Back Stitch

Cross Stitch (twice in 2 colors) + Cross Stitch

Cross Stitch + Straight Stitch

detached wheatear stitch combinations

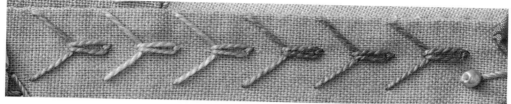

Detached Wheatear Stitch (in a row)

Detached Wheatear Stitch + Seed Beads

Detached Wheatear Stitch + French Knot

Detached Wheatear Stitch + Star Stitch

embroidered motifs

Straight Stitch + French Knot

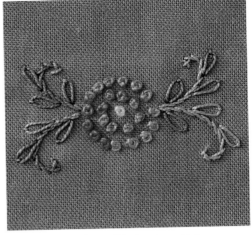

French Knot + Stem Stitch + Lazy Daisy

Stem Stitch + Straight Stitch + French Knot +
Lazy Daisy + silk ribbon bow (4mm silk
ribbon) + Seed Beads

Lazy Daisy + French Knot

Rosette Stitch + Lazy Daisy + Seed Beads

French Knot + Lazy Daisy

French Knot + Lazy Daisy + Chain-Stitch leaves

Lazy Daisy + Stem Stitch + French Knot

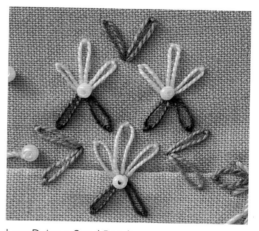

Lazy Daisy + Seed Beads

Lazy Daisy + Seed Beads

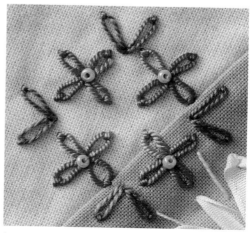

Lazy Daisy + Seed Beads

Blanket Stitch + Stem Stitch + Lazy Daisy

Blanket Stitch + Straight Stitch +
French Knot + Feather Stitch leaves

Fly Stitch + French Knot + Feather Stitch
leaves

Feather Stitch + French Knot

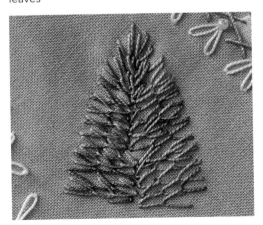

Feather Stitch

Stem Stitch + Ribbon Stitch (4 mm silk ribbon)

Stem Stitch + Ribbon Stitch (4 mm silk ribbon) + Seed Beads

Straight Stitch + Seed Beads

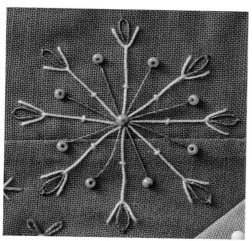

Fly Stitch + Couching Stitch + Straight Stitch + Lazy Daisy + Seed Beads

Straight Stitch + Chain Stitch + French Knot + Straight Stitch

Stem Stitch + Fly Stitch + French Knot + Colonial Knot Running Stitch Rose (7 mm silk ribbon) + Lazy Daisy

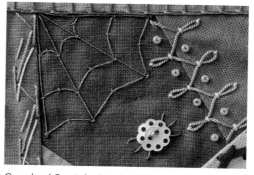

Couched Straight Stitch + Button + Straight Stitch

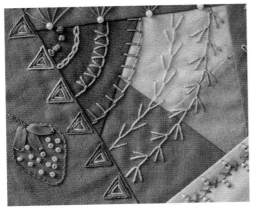

Feather Stitch—Knotted + Feather Stitch + Blanket Stitch + Blanket Stitch—Knotted + Chain Stitch + French Knot

Couched Straight Stitch + Feather Stitch + Blanket Stitch + Chain Stitch + silk ribbon bow (4 mm silk ribbon) + Seed Beads

Stem Stitch + Lazy Daisy + French Knot

French Knot + Lazy Daisy

Herringbone Stitch + Straight Stitch + Back Stitch + French Knot

Cross Stitch + Star Stitch

Fly Stitch + Straight Stitch + Lazy Daisy + Seed Beads

feather stitch combinations

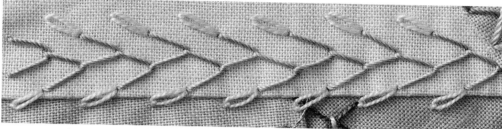

Feather Stitch + Lazy Daisy

Feather Stitch—Double + Lazy Daisy + Bullion Knot

Feather Stitch + Ribbon Stitch (4 mm silk ribbon)

Feather Stitch + Lazy Daisy + Ribbon Stitch (4 mm silk ribbon) + French Knot

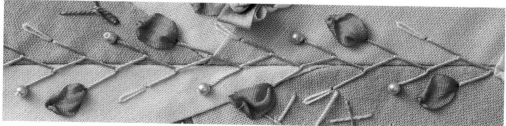

Feather Stitch + Lazy Daisy + Ribbon Stitch (7 mm silk ribbon) + Pearls

Feather Stitch + French Knot + Ribbon Stitch (7 mm silk ribbon)

Feather Stitch (2 mm silk ribbon and #12 perle cotton)

Feather Stitch (2 mm silk ribbon) + Lazy Daisy (4 mm silk ribbon)

Feather Stitch (2 mm silk ribbon) + Loop Flower (4 mm silk ribbon) + French Knot (4 mm silk ribbon)

Feather Stitch—Double + Plume Stitch (4 mm silk ribbon) + Pearls

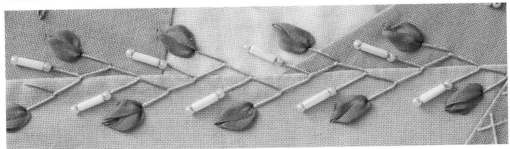

Feather Stitch—Double + Lazy Daisy (4 mm silk ribbon) + Bugle Beads + Seed Beads

Feather Stitch—Triple + Lazy Daisy + Seed Beads

Feather Stitch—Knotted + Seed Beads

Feather Stitch + Lazy Daisy + Oval Beads + Seed Beads

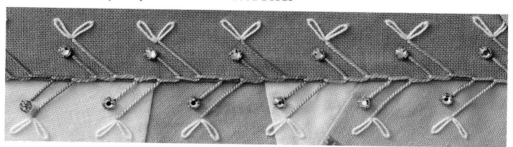

Feather Stitch + Lazy Daisy + Rose Montées

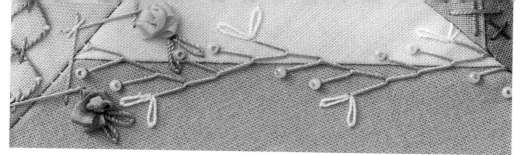

Feather Stitch + Pearls

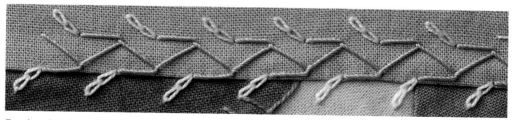

Feather Stitch + Chain Stitch

Feather Stitch + French Knot (7 mm silk ribbon) + Ribbon Stitch (4 mm silk ribbon) + Seed Beads

Feather Stitch + Lazy Daisy + Seed Beads

Feather Stitch + Glass Flower Beads + Seed Beads

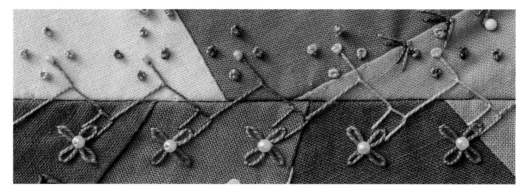

Feather Stitch + French Knot + Lazy Daisy + Pearls

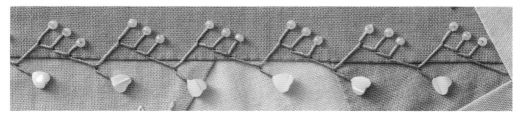

Feather Stitch + Heart Beads + Seed Beads

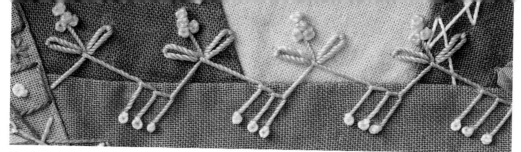

Feather Stitch + Lazy Daisy + French Knot

Feather Stitch + Lazy Daisy + Rosette Stitch

Feather Stitch + Back Stitch + Lazy Daisy

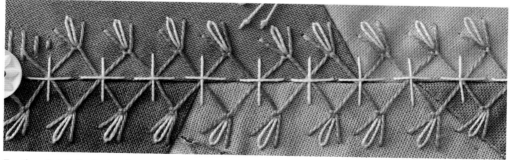

Feather Stitch (twice) + Cross Stitch + Lazy Daisy

Curved Feather Stitch + Seed Beads

Curved Feather Stitch + Seed Beads

Curved Feather Stitch + Glass Flower Beads + Seed Beads + Ribbon Stitch (7 mm silk ribbon)

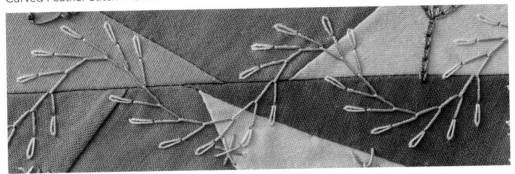

Curved Feather Stitch + Lazy Daisy

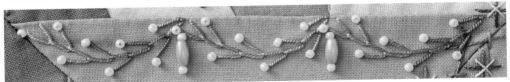

Feather Stitch + Seed Beads + Oval Beads

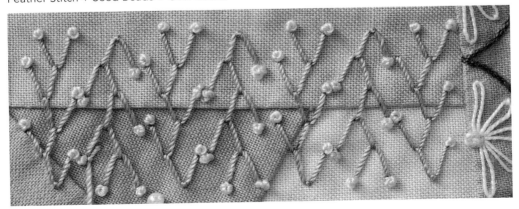

Horizontal Feather Stitch + French Knot

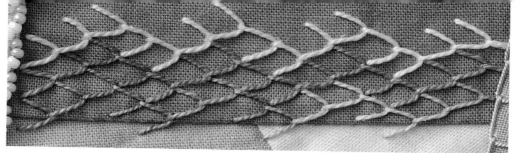

Feather Stitch—Double (3 times)

Feather Stitch branch + Ribbon Stitch
(4 mm silk ribbon) + Seed Beads

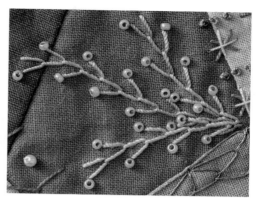

Feather Stitch branch + Seed Beads

Feather Stitch branch + Plume Stitch (4 mm silk
ribbon) + Seed Beads

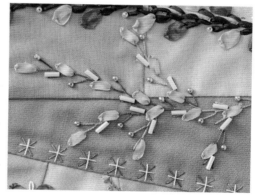

Feather Stitch branch + Ribbon Stitch
(4 mm silk ribbon) + Pearls + Bugle Beads

fly stitch combinations

Fly Stitch + French Knot

Fly Stitch + French Knot

Fly Stitch + French Knot + Seed Beads

Stacked Fly Stitch + Seed Beads

Fly Stitch (twice)

Fly Stitch + Seed Beads

Fly Stitch (twice)

Fly Stitch + Lazy Daisy + Pearls

Fly Stitch + Lazy Daisy

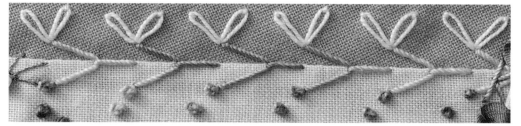

Fly Stitch + Lazy Daisy + French Knot

Fly Stitch + Lazy Daisy + Seed Beads

Fly Stitch + French Knot + Ribbon Stitch (7 mm silk ribbon)

Fly Stitch (twice) + Lazy Daisy (4 mm silk ribbon and thread)

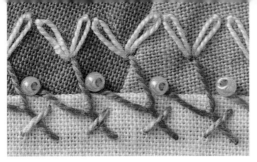

Fly Stitch + Lazy Daisy + Straight Stitch + Seed Beads

Fly Stitch + Lazy Daisy + Straight Stitch + Back Stitch + Seed Beads

Fly Stitch + Pearls

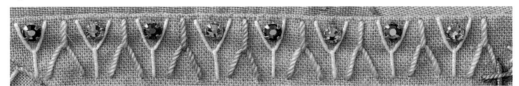

Fly Stitch + Rose Montées

Fly Stitch + Lazy Daisy + French Knot

Fly Stitch + Lazy Daisy (4 mm silk ribbon)

Fly Stitch + Ribbon Stitch (7 mm silk ribbon)

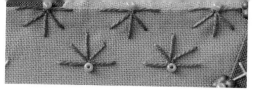

Fly Stitch + Straight Stitch + Seed Beads

Fly Stitch snowflakes

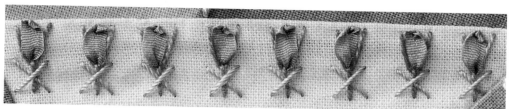

Fly Stitch + Cross Stitch + Ribbon Stitch (4 mm silk ribbon)

Fly Stitch (twice) + Lazy Daisy + Oval Beads

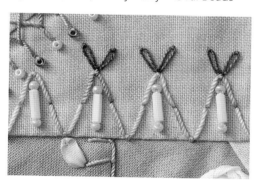

Fly Stitch (twice) + Lazy Daisy + Bugle Beads + Seed Beads

Fly Stitch + French Knot

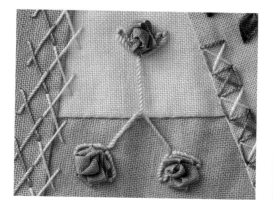

Fly Stitch + Lazy Daisy + Colonial Knot Running Stitch Rose (4 mm silk ribbon)

Fly Stitch + Straight Stitch + Lazy Daisy + Sequin Flower + Seed Beads

french knot combinations

French Knot

French Knot (twice)

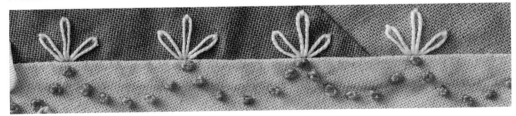

French Knot + Glass Flower Beads + Seed Beads

French Knot + Lazy Daisy

French Knot

French Knot + Ribbon Stitch (4 mm silk ribbon)

French Knot + Lazy Daisy

herringbone stitch combinations

Herringbone Stitch (2mm silk ribbon)

Herringbone Stitch + Seed Beads

Herringbone Stitch + Cross Stitch

Herringbone Stitch (2 colors)

Stacked Herringbone Stitch

Herringbone Stitch + Lazy Daisy

Herringbone Stitch (twice) + Pearls

Herringbone Stitch + Straight Stitch + Seed Beads

Herringbone Stitch + Lazy Daisy + Seed Beads

Herringbone Stitch + Pistil Stitch + Seed Beads

Herringbone Stitch + Straight Stitch + Seed Beads

Herringbone Stitch + Fly Stitch + Seed Beads

Herringbone Stitch + Back Stitch + Straight Stitch + Seed Beads

Herringbone Stitch + Blanket Stitch—Fan + Pearls + Seed Beads

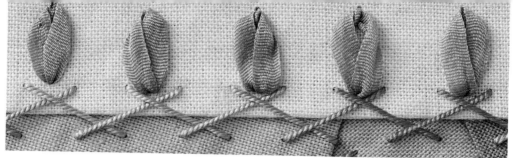

Herringbone Stitch + Lazy Daisy (4 mm silk ribbon)

Herringbone Stitch + Colonial Knot Running Stitch Rose (4 mm silk ribbon) + Lazy Daisy + Straight Stitch

Herringbone Stitch + Ribbon Stitch (7 mm and 4 mm silk ribbon)

High-Low Herringbone Stitch + Lazy Daisy + Seed Beads

High-Low Herringbone Stitch + Straight Stitch + Glass Flower Beads + Seed Beads

Detached Herringbone Stitch + Lazy Daisy (4 mm silk ribbon)

Detached Herringbone Stitch + Sequin Flowers + Seed Beads + Straight Stitch

Detached Herringbone Stitch + Straight Stitch + Rose Montées + Seed Beads

Detached Herringbone Stitch + Cross Stitch + Straight Stitch + Glass Flower Beads + Seed Beads

Detached Herringbone Stitch + Straight Stitch + Sequin Flowers + Seed Beads

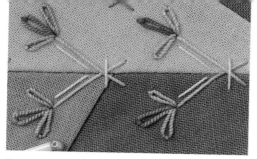

Detached Herringbone Stitch + Lazy Daisy + Straight Stitch

Detached Herringbone Stitch + Cross Stitch + Straight Stitch + Back Stitch

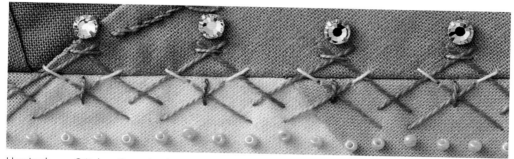

Herringbone Stitch + Detached Herringbone Stitch + Straight Stitch + Rose Montées + Seed Beads

Herringbone Stitch + Straight Stitch

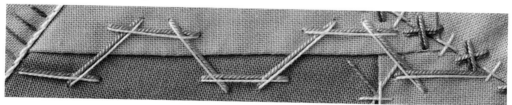

Herringbone Stitch (twice)

Herringbone Stitch + Colonial Knot Running Stitch Rose (7 mm silk ribbon) + Lazy Daisy (2 mm silk ribbon)

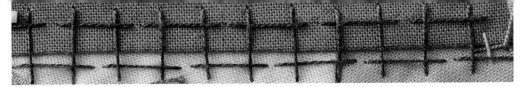

Herringbone Stitch picket fence

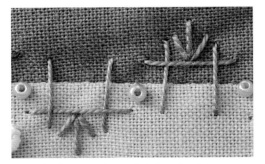

Detached Herringbone Stitch + Straight
Stitch + Seed Beads

Detached Herringbone Stitch + Lazy Daisy +
Sequin Flowers + Seed Beads

Herringbone Stitch + Straight Stitch + Back Stitch

Herringbone Stitch + Star Stitch

Herringbone Stitch—Back Stitched + Lazy Daisy + Straight Stitch

Herringbone Stitch—Back Stitched + Straight Stitch + Seed Beads

Stacked Herringbone Stitch—Back Stitched + Seed Beads

Herringbone Stitch + Fly Stitch + Straight Stitch

Herringbone Stitch + Straight Stitch

Herringbone Stitch + Star Stitch + Straight Stitch

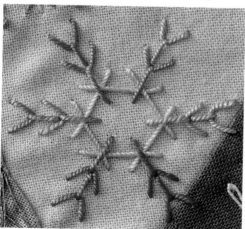

Herringbone Stitch + Fly Stitch

laced stitch combinations

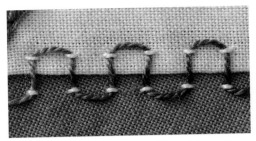

Small Straight Stitch + thread laced through Straight Stitch

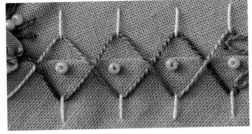

Large Straight Stitch + thread laced through Straight Stitch (twice) + Seed Beads

Small Straight Stitch + thread laced through Straight Stitch + Straight Stitch

Small Straight Stitch + thread laced through Straight Stitch + Seed Beads

Straight Stitch + thread laced through Straight Stitch + Seed Beads

Cretan Stitch + thread laced through Cretan Stitch

Fly Stitch + thread laced through Fly Stitch

Herringbone Stitch + Seed Beads + thread laced through Herringbone Stitch

lazy daisy combinations

Lazy Daisy + Seed Beads

Lazy Daisy + Pistil Stitch + Seed Beads

Lazy Daisy + French Knot

Lazy Daisy + Pistil Stitch + French Knot

Lazy Daisy + Straight Stitch + Seed Beads

Lazy Daisy + Straight Stitch + French Knot
(7 mm silk ribbon and thread)

Lazy Daisy + Stem Stitch + French Knot

Lazy Daisy + French Knot + Straight Stitch

leaf stitch combinations

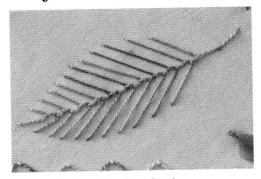

Feather Stitch + Couching Stitch

Feather Stitch (2 mm silk ribbon)

Cretan Stitch + Couching Stitch

Fly Stitch + Couching Stitch

Blanket Stitch (twice) + Couching Stitch

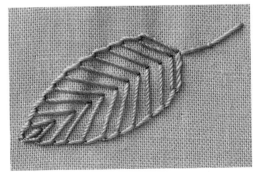

Blanket Stitch (twice) + Couched Straight Stitch

Blanket Stitch + Stem Stitch + Seed Beads

Lazy Daisy + Couched Straight Stitch

Stem Stitch + French Knot

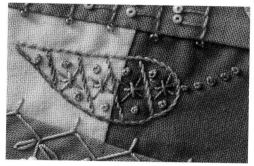

Stem Stitch + Star Stitch + French Knot

Stem Stitch + Chain Stitch—Feathered

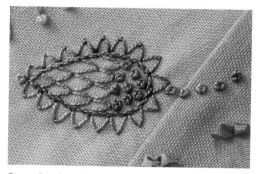

Stem Stitch + Fly Stitch + French Knot

Chain Stitch + French Knot

Chain Stitch + Herringbone Stitch +
Stem Stitch (twice) + French Knot

sheaf stitch combinations

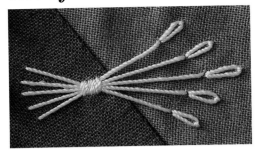

Sheaf Stitch + Lazy Daisy

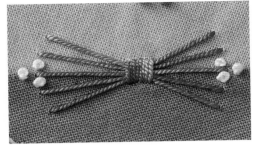

Sheaf Stitch + French Knot

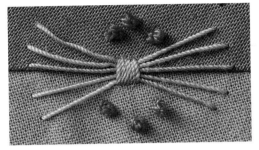

Sheaf Stitch + French Knot

Sheaf Stitch + Star Stitch

Sheaf Stitch (thread and 7 mm silk ribbon) +
French Knot + Seed Bead

Sheaf Stitch + Straight Stitch + Lazy Daisy +
Seed Beads

Sheaf Stitch + Lazy Daisy

Sheaf Stitch + Lazy Daisy

silk ribbon embroidery stitch combinations

Ribbon Stitch (7 mm silk ribbon) + Pearls + Feather Stitch leaves

Ribbon Stitch (7 mm silk ribbon) + Lazy Daisy + French Knot (7 mm silk ribbon)

Straight Stitch (7 mm silk ribbon) + French Knot (7 mm silk ribbon) + Lazy Daisy (7 mm silk ribbon)

Straight Stitch (7 mm silk ribbon and thread) + French Knot (7 mm silk ribbon) + Ribbon Stitch (7 mm silk ribbon)

Ribbon Stitch (twice in 4 mm silk ribbon) + French Knot + Feather Stitch leaves

Ribbon Stitch (7 mm silk ribbon) + Pearls

Side Ribbon Stitch Flower (7 mm silk ribbon) +
French Knot (7 mm silk ribbon)

Blanket Stitch—Circular + Ribbon Stitch
(7 mm silk ribbon) + Pearl

Colonial Knot (7 mm silk ribbon) + Straight Stitch (7 mm silk ribbon) + Pearls

Colonial Knot (7 mm silk ribbon) + Straight Stitch (7 mm silk ribbon) + Colonial Knot Running
Stitch Rose (4 mm silk ribbon)

Ribbon Stitch (7 mm silk ribbon) + Bugle
Bead + Running Stitch + Pistil Stitch

Lazy Daisy (4 mm silk ribbon) + Bullion Knot +
Pistil Stitch

Spider Web Rose (7 mm silk ribbon) +
Ribbon Stitch (7 mm silk ribbon)

Spider Web Rose (7 mm silk ribbon) + Side Ribbon Stitch Flower (7 mm silk ribbon) + Lazy Daisy (7 mm silk ribbon)

French Knot (4 mm silk ribbon) + Ribbon Stitch (7 mm silk ribbon)

French Knot (4 mm silk ribbon) + Ribbon Stitch (7 mm silk ribbon) + Straight Stitch

French Knot (4 mm silk ribbon) + Ribbon Stitch (7 mm silk ribbon) + Side Ribbon Stitch Flower (7 mm silk ribbon) + Straight Stitch

Ribbon Stitch (7 mm silk ribbon) + Side Ribbon Stitch Flower (7 mm silk ribbon) + Ribbon Stitch (4 mm silk ribbon) + Stem Stitch

French Knot (4 mm silk ribbon)+ Ribbon Stitch (7 mm silk ribbon) + Stem Stitch (4 mm silk ribbon)

Loop Flower (7 mm silk ribbon) + Glass Flower + Seed Bead + Feather Stitch leaves

Loop Flower (twice in 7 mm silk ribbon) + French Knot (4 mm silk ribbon) + Ribbon Stitch (7 mm silk ribbon)

Bullion Knot / Lazy Daisy Combination Stitch (4 mm silk ribbon) + French Knot (4 mm silk ribbon)

Bullion Knot / Lazy Daisy Combination Stitch (4 mm silk ribbon) + Lazy Daisy (4 mm silk ribbon) + Pistil Stitch

Straight Stitch (4 mm silk ribbon) + Stem Stitch + Straight Stitch

Spider Web Rose (7 mm silk ribbon) + Feather Stitch

Stem Stitch Rose (4 mm silk ribbon) +
Ribbon Stitch (7 mm silk ribbon)

Chain-Stitch Rose (4 mm silk ribbon) +
Feather Stitch leaves

Straight Stitch (4 mm silk ribbon) + Seed Beads

Colonial Knot Running Stitch Rose (7 mm silk
ribbon) + Ribbon Stitch (7 mm silk ribbon)

Lazy Daisy (4 mm silk ribbon) + Straight
Stitch + French Knot + Ribbon Stitch (7 mm silk
ribbon)

Spider Web Rose (2 colors of 4 mm silk
ribbon) + Bullion Knot / Lazy Daisy
Combination Stitch leaves (4 mm silk ribbon)

Stem Stitch (4 mm silk ribbon) + Loop Flowers
(4 mm silk ribbon) + French Knot (4 mm silk
ribbon) + Lazy Daisy (4 mm silk ribbon)

star stitch combinations

Star Stitch (1 color)

Star Stitch (2 colors)

Star Stitch + Straight Stitch + French Knot

Star Stitch + French Knot + Straight Stitch

Star Stitch + French Knot

Star Stitch (in a V shape)

Star Stitch + Cross Stitch + Lazy Daisy +
French Knot

Star Stitch + Feather Stitch + Pearls

stem stitch combinations

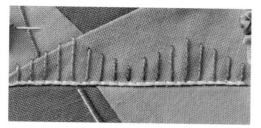

Stem Stitch + Straight Stitch

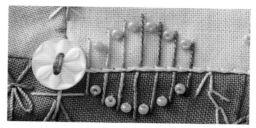

Stem Stitch + Straight Stitch + Seed Beads

Stem Stitch + Lazy Daisy + Oval Pearls

Stem Stitch + Lazy Daisy + Colonial Knot Running Stitch Rose (4 mm silk ribbon)

Stem Stitch + Lazy Daisy + Bullion Knot rose + Ribbon Stitch (4 mm silk ribbon)

Stem Stitch + Straight Stitch + Button

Stem Stitch + Straight Stitch

Stem Stitch + Lazy Daisy + French Knot

Stem Stitch + Feather Stitch + Oval Pearls

Stem Stitch + Lazy Daisy

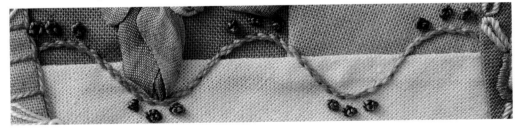

Stem Stitch + French Knot

Stem Stitch + Star Stitch + French Knot

Stem Stitch + French Knot

Stem Stitch + French Knot + Lazy Daisy

Stem Stitch + Feather Stitch + Fly Stitch

Stem Stitch + Lazy Daisy + French Knot

Stem Stitch + Blanket Stitch + Seed Beads

Stem Stitch + Spider Web Rose (4mm silk ribbon) + Ribbon Stitch (4mm silk ribbon) + Lazy Daisy (4mm silk ribbon)

Stem Stitch + Seed Beads + Lazy Daisy

Stem Stitch + Straight Stitch (4mm silk ribbon) + Seed Beads

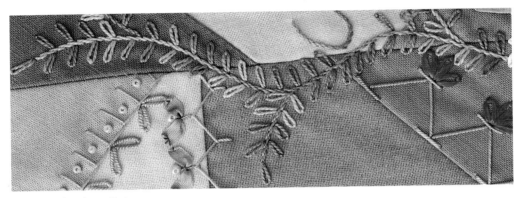

Stem Stitch + Lazy Daisy

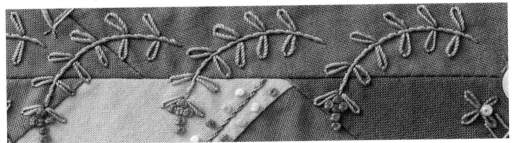

Stem Stitch + Lazy Daisy + French Knot

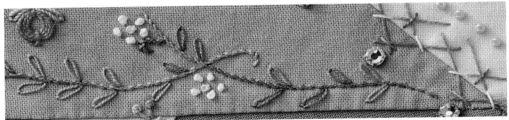

Stem Stitch + Lazy Daisy + French Knot

Stem Stitch + French Knot

Stem Stitch ("Love") + Lazy Daisy + French Knot

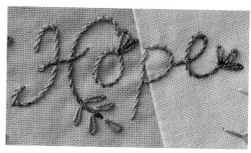

Stem Stitch ("Hope") + Lazy Daisy

Stem Stitch ("Grace") + French Knot

Stem Stitch ("Joy")

Stem Stitch ("B") + Lazy Daisy + French Knot

Stem Stitch ("V") + French Knot

Stem Stitch + French Knot

Stem Stitch + Cross Stitch + French Knot

Stem Stitch

Stem Stitch + Cross Stitch + Straight Stitch +
Back Stitch

Stem Stitch + French Knot

Stem Stitch + French Knot + Lazy Daisy

straight-stitch combinations

Straight Stitch

Straight Stitch

Straight Stitch

Straight Stitch + Seed Beads

Straight Stitch + French Knot

Couched Straight Stitch + Straight Stitch +
Back Stitch

Couched Straight Stitch + Straight Stitch +
Back Stitch

Straight Stitch + French Knot

Straight Stitch + Glass Flower Beads + Seed Beads

Straight Stitch + Lazy Daisy + Seed Beads

Straight Stitch + French Knot

Straight Stitch + French Knot

combination group stitches

Blanket/Cretan Combination Stitch + Straight Stitch + Oval Beads

Cretan/Herringbone Combination Stitch + Straight Stitch + Buttons

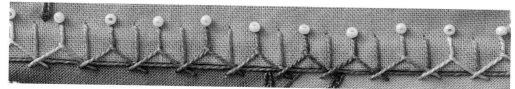

Blanket Stitch + Cretan/Herringbone Combination Stitch + Seed Beads

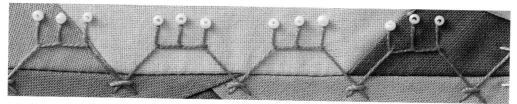

Blanket/Herringbone Combination Stitch + Straight Stitch + Seed Beads

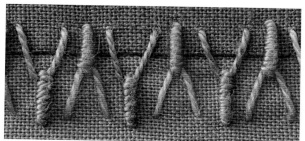

Bullion Knot/Fly Stitch Combination Stitch

Bullion Knot/Lazy Daisy Combination Stitch + Straight Stitch + French Knot

Stitch Patterns

Leaf

Feather Stitch
Tree

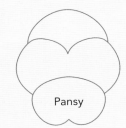

Pansy

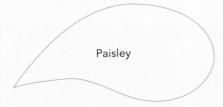

Paisley

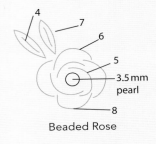

Beaded Rose

Music

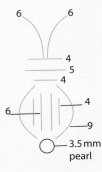

Beaded Bunny

Beaded
Feather Stitch Leaf

INSTRUCTIONS:

First 3 stitches:
Use 6 beads.

Next 2 stitches:
Use 8 beads.

Next 4 stitches:
Use 10 beads.

Next stitch:
Use 8 beads.

Last stitch:
Use 6 beads.

Stem:
Use 11 beads.

For Bullion Knot rose + Lazy Daisy (page 76) and for Bullion Knot rose + Straight Stitch + French Knot (page 77), do 6 wraps for the center Bullion Knot and 9 wraps for the Bullion Knots on either side.

For Bullion Knot rose + Stem Stitch + Lazy Daisy leaves + Straight Stitch + Seed Beads (page 77), do 6 wraps for the center Bullion Knot and 9 wraps for the outer Bullion Knots.

For Bullion Knot rose + Lazy Daisy + French Knot (page 77), do 11 wraps for the 2 center Bullion Knots and 14 wraps for the remaining Bullion Knots.

For Bullion Knot rose + Feather Stitch leaves (page 77), do 12 wraps for the center 4 Bullion Knots, 25 wraps for the 4 Bullion Knots in the second layer, and 27 wraps for the 4 Bullion Knots in the outer layer of the rose.

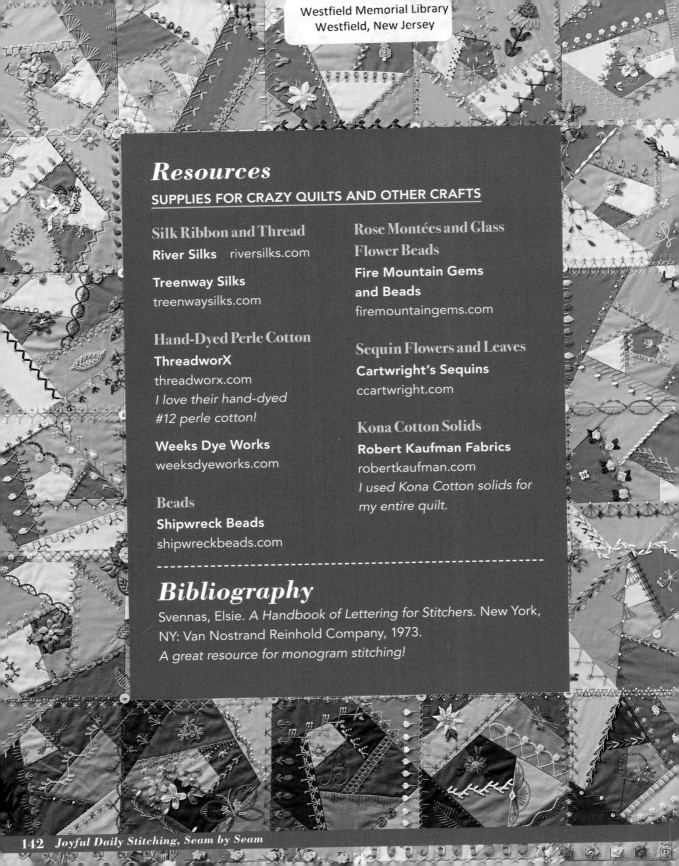

Resources

SUPPLIES FOR CRAZY QUILTS AND OTHER CRAFTS

Silk Ribbon and Thread

River Silks   riversilks.com

Treenway Silks
treenwaysilks.com

Hand-Dyed Perle Cotton

ThreadworX
threadworx.com
*I love their hand-dyed
#12 perle cotton!*

Weeks Dye Works
weeksdyeworks.com

Beads

Shipwreck Beads
shipwreckbeads.com

Rose Montées and Glass Flower Beads

**Fire Mountain Gems
and Beads**
firemountaingems.com

Sequin Flowers and Leaves

Cartwright's Sequins
ccartwright.com

Kona Cotton Solids

Robert Kaufman Fabrics
robertkaufman.com
*I used Kona Cotton solids for
my entire quilt.*

Bibliography

Svennas, Elsie. *A Handbook of Lettering for Stitchers*. New York,
NY: Van Nostrand Reinhold Company, 1973.
A great resource for monogram stitching!